UNDERSTANDING "I"

Lines of Thought

Short philosophical books

Published in association with the Aristotelian Society

Series editor: Scott Sturgeon

Hume Variations
Jerry A. Fodor

Moral Fictionalism
Mark Eli Kalderon

Perfectionism and the Common Good: Themes in the Philosophy of T. H. Green
David O. Brink

Knowledge and Practical Interests
Jason Stanley

Thought and Reality
Michael Dummett

Our Knowledge of the Internal World
Robert C. Stalnaker

Mental Files in Flux
François Recanati

Understanding "I": Language and Thought
José Luis Bermúdez

UNDERSTANDING "I"

Language and Thought

JOSÉ LUIS BERMÚDEZ

UNIVERSITY PRESS

Great Clarendon Street, Oxford, OX2 6DP,
United Kingdom

Oxford University Press is a department of the University of Oxford.
It furthers the University's objective of excellence in research, scholarship,
and education by publishing worldwide. Oxford is a registered trade mark of
Oxford University Press in the UK and in certain other countries

© José Luis Bermúdez 2016

The moral rights of the author have been asserted

First Edition published in 2016

Impression: 1

All rights reserved. No part of this publication may be reproduced, stored in
a retrieval system, or transmitted, in any form or by any means, without the
prior permission in writing of Oxford University Press, or as expressly permitted
by law, by licence or under terms agreed with the appropriate reprographics
rights organization. Enquiries concerning reproduction outside the scope of the
above should be sent to the Rights Department, Oxford University Press, at the
address above

You must not circulate this work in any other form
and you must impose this same condition on any acquirer

Published in the United States of America by Oxford University Press
198 Madison Avenue, New York, NY 10016, United States of America

British Library Cataloguing in Publication Data

Data available

Library of Congress Control Number: 2016952219

ISBN 978–0–19–879621–3

Printed in Great Britain by
Clays Ltd, St Ives plc

Links to third party websites are provided by Oxford in good faith and
for information only. Oxford disclaims any responsibility for the materials
contained in any third party website referenced in this work.

Preface

I have been working on self-consciousness and self-awareness for over twenty years. Much of my work in this area has taken as target the widely held view that the distinguishing mark of self-conscious thought is the ability to speak and think about oneself using the first-person pronoun "I" and comparable linguistic devices. In *The Paradox of Self-Consciousness* and subsequent work I argued that the full-fledged self-consciousness that comes with linguistic self-reference emerges from a rich foundation of nonconceptual self-consciousness, available to nonlinguistic animals and prelinguistic infants as well as to language-using humans.

My primary emphasis has been, as it were, on the part of the iceberg that lies beneath the surface—on the ways in which animals, human and nonhuman, receive and exploit distinctively self-specifying forms of information that allow them to think nonconceptually about themselves. Such information comes from a range of sources. We find it in somatic proprioception and kinesthesis, for example, which provide body-relative information, including information about limb position and movement. Ordinary "outward-directed" perception carries a great deal of information about the perceiver's own location and trajectory, while basic navigational abilities exploit the intimate connection between awareness of one's own egocentric route through the environment and awareness of allocentric spatial relations between landmarks. That there are such nonconceptual forms of self-consciousness seems now to be much more widely accepted than it was in 1998 when I published *The Paradox of Self-Consciousness* and the late Susan Hurley published her book *Consciousness in Action*, which contained a similarly motivated discussion.

The focus of this book is the visible part of the iceberg—the various forms of full-fledged self-conscious thought that are typically expressed with the first person pronoun. The aim is to elucidate the unique psychological role that self-conscious thoughts (typically expressed using "I") play in action and cognition—a unique role often summarized by describing "I" as an essential indexical. Chapter 1 explains and defends this way of thinking about "I" against a challenge raised by Herman Cappelen and Josh Dever in their book *The Inessential Indexical*. Using the framework proposed by Cappelen and Dever I show that, even on their own terms, psychological explanations have to be indexical. This argument sets the agenda for the book. Sentences using "I" express first person thoughts. Those thoughts have a distinctive role, evidenced by but not restricted to, their role in motivating action. Explaining how we understand the first person pronoun is one way of explaining what first person thoughts are and how they work.

Elucidating conceptual self-consciousness might seem easier than elucidating nonconceptual self-consciousness, because of the close connections between "I"-thoughts and the "I"-sentences that express them. However, dominant models in the philosophy of language, which treat "I" as a directly referential term, seem unsuited to the task of explaining how we understand "I." Fortunately, as emerges in Chapter 2, a directly referential approach to the semantics of "I" is perfectly compatible with, and arguably requires, a substantive account of what it is to understand sentences involving the first person pronoun. The account of linguistic understanding that I propose is Fregean in inspiration, elucidating understanding in terms of sense and sense in terms of grasping the truth conditions of sentences.

Frege's own remarks on the sense of "I" are schematic at best. As we see in Chapter 3, the most developed Fregean account has been offered by Gareth Evans in *The Varieties of Reference*. Evans applies his basic principle that understanding referring expressions involves standing in, and being able to act directly upon, *information-links* to the referent of the expression. The information-sources he emphasizes include those discussed above as particularly important for nonconceptual self-consciousness. They typically give rise to judgments that are *immune to error through misidentification relative to the first person pronoun* because they are uniquely about the self in such a way that no identification of a particular object is required, and hence there is no possibility of misidentification. The second (output) component of his account emphasizes the direct implications of "I"-thoughts for action (as in the thesis of essential indexicality). The third component of his account (the objectivity component) ties mastery of "I" to the ability to locate oneself in an objective spatio-temporal world, to integrate one's egocentric path through the world with a cognitive map that is perspective-free.

For Frege: "Everyone is presented to himself in a special and primitive way, in which he is presented to no-one else." He accepts the consequence that the sense of "I" is private and incommunicable. Evans follows him in accepting privacy, while arguing that unshareable "I"-thoughts can nonetheless be objective. Chapter 4 rejects this argument and offers a positive argument for what I term the *Symmetry Constraint*: An account of the sense of "I" must allow tokens of "I" to have the same sense as tokens of other personal pronouns such as "you" in appropriate contexts. In certain contexts, not terribly unusual, the very same (token) thought can be expressed by me using "I" and by you using "you." The Symmetry Constraint is motivated in three ways: (a) semantically, through considerations of same-saying and reported speech; (b) logically, in terms of when speakers should be counted as contradicting each other; (c) epistemologically, in order to allow paradigm instances of testimony to count as knowledge.

The Symmetry Constraint allows for token-equivalence in sense between a token of "I" and, for example, a token of "you." But at another level, understanding how to use the first person pronoun "I" is plainly a very different matter from understanding how to use the second person pronoun "you." So, Chapter 5 shows, we need to distinguish (at least in the case of "I" and other indexical expressions, such as "now" and "here":

The token-sense of "I": What a speaker or hearer understands when they utter or hear a token utterance involving "I";

The type-sense of "I": That in virtue of which a speaker or hearer can properly be said to understand and know how to use the linguistic expression "I."

This distinction cannot be mapped onto standard distinctions made in discussions of "I" (and other indexicals)—for example, Kaplan's distinction between character and content and Perry's distinction between content-M, content-C, and content-D. Neither does what a satisfactory account of token-sense must do, namely, respect both Frege's criterion for sameness/difference of sense (particularly with respect to coreferential proper names) and the Symmetry Constraint.

Chapter 6 develops my positive account of the sense of "I." The type-sense of "I" is relatively straightforward: Mark Sainsbury's suggestion that "I" is the expression that English speakers use to refer to themselves as themselves. Token-sense is more complicated. Rejecting the privacy and unshareability of "I"-thoughts means that the token-sense of "I" cannot be explained in terms of sensitivity to distinctive kinds of information, as Evans proposed. I propose that we think about the token-sense of "I" in terms of the third component in Evans's account. The token-sense of "I" is given by the thinker's ability to think of herself as an object uniquely located in space and following a unique trajectory through space-time. This knowledge is a practical capacity—the capacity to situate onself within a cognitive map of the world, achieved by the thinker superimposing her egocentric understanding of space upon a non-egocentric representation of how the environment is spatially configured.

I show how my account of the sense of "I" meets five constraints upon a satisfactory account of the sense of "I" that have emerged from the earlier discussion. The account shows how the sense of "I" can be shareable. It shows how the Symmetry Constraint can be met in certain circumstances (and explains why it fails to hold in other circumstances). And it accommodates the general distinction between knowing in general terms what it would be for the sentence featuring the indexical to be true (without necessarily being able to identify the referent of the indexical) and knowing a specific truth condition (where this requires being able to identify the referents of the indexical). Moreover, the self-locating abilities I discuss are at the root of the phenomenon of Essential Indexicality. The knowledge typically acquired in the cases that illustrate the phenomenon of essential indexicality is self-locating knowledge, exactly as one would expect if the sense of "I" is understood as proposed here.

Nonetheless, my account of the token-sense of "I" poses an important challenge: Is there a way of explaining the sense of first person judgments that are immune to error through misidentification, now that we have cut the connection between the sense of "I," on the one hand, and sensitivity to information-sources giving rise to those judgments? The first part of the chapter shows how a large class of first person judgments with the immunity property can be understood in terms of the possession conditions for the non-indexical concepts. Concepts that can be applied to oneself on the basis of information-sources that are immune to error through misidentification have both first and third person clauses in their possession conditions. The first person clause explains how judgments in which those concepts feature can be based on "private" information sources (such as introspection, somatic proprioception, and visual kinesthesis). The third person clause explains how judgments with the IEM property can be shareable.

This general strategy will not work, however, for past-tense judgments that are based upon autobiographical memory without being explicit memory judgments. Many (but not all) such judgments have the immunity property but, since they can deploy almost any

Preface ~ ix

concept in the thinker's conceptual repertoire, it is most implausible that many concepts have a special clause in their possession conditions for applications based on autobiographical memory. I argue that past-tense judgments have the IEM property when and only when the original experience(s) in which they are based are such that, had a present-tense judgment been made at the time at which they occurred, that present-tense judgment would have had the immunity property. Autobiographical memory is very different from introspection or proprioception. It is not itself an information channel that confers the immunity property, but rather a mode of transmitting that property.

I am particularly grateful for comments on a draft of this manuscript from two readers for Oxford University Press (one of whom subsequently revealed himself to be Michael Rescorla), as well as from audiences at the Department of Philosophy at UC Santa Barbara; the Berlin School of Mind and Brain; the Department of Philosophy at the University of Córdoba, Argentina; the Center for Subjectivity Research at the University of Copenhagen; and the Institute of Philosophy at the University of Warsaw.

I have drawn upon material from the articles listed in the Bibliography as Bermúdez 2005b, 2011a, 2012, 2013, and forthcoming-a. I am very grateful for permission from Oxford University Press, the editors and publisher of *Grazer Philosophische Studien*, and the Analysis Trust for the reuse of this material.

Contents

List of Figures	xiii
1. "I": An Essential Indexical	1
2. Sense and Understanding	20
3. Frege and Evans on the Sense of "I"	42
4. Privacy, Objectivity, Symmetry	61
5. Token-Sense and Type-Sense	80
6. "I": Token-Sense and Type-Sense	97
7. Explaining Immunity to Error through Misidentification	128
References	151
Index	159

List of Figures

2.1 A schematic representation of how my utterance of the sentence "I am F" would be interpreted on a Fregean model of language, as standardly understood in contemporary philosophy of language.   23

2.2 A schematic representation of how my utterance of the sentence "I am F" would be interpreted on the Russell/Mill model of language, as standardly understood in contemporary philosophy of language.   24

2.3 A more accurate depiction of the Fregean model of sense, incorporating the dimension of understanding and the idea that sense is a mode of presentation of reference.   29

2.4 The hybrid view, which is the Russell/Mill model expanded to incorporate a Fregean account of linguistic understanding in terms of sense.   30

7.1 A schematic representation of the relations of warrant and grounding in past-tense memory judgments based on autobiographical memory.   141

I
"I": An Essential Indexical

No words in English are shorter than "I" and few, if any, play a more fundamental role in language and thought. "I" allows speakers to refer to themselves. Through the device of self-reference, speakers can describe themselves physically and psychologically. They can express both their momentary desires and their long-term goals. And they can articulate their view of where they stand in the world, literally and metaphorically. They can, in other words, think "I"-thoughts.

One might think that these linguistic achievements make it possible for speakers to think about themselves in a special way—to think about themselves self-consciously. Self-conscious thinkers are certainly conscious of the world, both the physical world and the social world. But they are also conscious of themselves, and conscious of the relation between themselves and the physical/social worlds. On this view, learning the linguistic device of self-reference opens cognitive doors. Being able to use "I" is a necessary condition for *thinking* "I"-thoughts.

On the other hand, one might think that the direction of acquisition goes the other way, so that the capacity for self-conscious thought is a necessary preliminary to linguistic self-reference. All that a child acquires on learning the personal pronoun "I" is the ability to express self-conscious thoughts that they were perfectly capable of thinking before they had the linguistic machinery to express them. On this view, learning the linguistic device of self-reference only opens communicative doors. Being able to use "I" just makes it possible to *express* "I"-thoughts.

This raises general questions about the direction of explanation between language and thought. These general questions are highly complex and have been much discussed. I have explored them in the specific context of self-reference and self-consciousness in my book *The Paradox of Self-Consciousness*. In this book, however, they will be set to one side. My guiding principle is that when we are dealing with self-conscious subjects who are competent users of "I," there is a single set of abilities underlying both self-conscious thought and self-referential language. The motivation for this guiding principle is set out in section 1.1. Section 1.2 explores how "I" functions in language and thought, focusing in particular on the by-now-familiar idea that action has an *essentially indexical* dimension, with "I"-thoughts playing a crucial and ineliminable role in both motivating and explaining action. Familiar though it may be, the thesis of essential indexicality is more often motivated through intuition and example than directly argued for. Section 1.3 provides such an argument.

1.1. *Language, Thought, and Expressibility*

In looking at the relation between self-reference in language and self-consciousness in thought I shall be guided by the following principle.

> THE EXPRESSIBILITY PRINCIPLE
> Any thinkable thought can in principle be linguistically expressed without residue or remainder.

A qualification. The Expressibility Principle is confined to the domain of conceptual content. It is not intended to apply to nonconceptual contents, typically taken to be perceptual in nature. There may be ineffable and inexpressible perceptual states. But if such there be, they are not counterexamples to the Expressibility Principle.

The Expressibility Principle is a general claim about thoughts and their linguistic expressibility, rather than a claim about individual thinkers or specific thoughts. It does not require, of any individual thinker, that she be able linguistically to express any thought that she might be able to think. Nor does it require of any thinkable thought that it either should have been expressed or will be expressed. What it says is that any thinkable thought is in principle linguistically expressible, so that the boundaries of thought cannot outstrip the boundaries of language.[1]

The Expressibility Principle is not saying that there are no inexpressible truths. What it says is that there can be no truths (or falsehoods, for that matter) that can be thought but not expressed. There may be inexpressible truths.[2] But if there are, they must also be unthinkable. There is no category of propositions that are thinkable but ineffable.

The Expressibility Principle is compatible with the plain fact that language and thought are both highly context-sensitive. It is a popular view that context-sensitive sentences are disambiguated at the level of thought. So, for example, what disambiguates my highly context-sensitive utterance of "I am going to the bank" is my intention to refer to myself and my intention to refer to the side of a river rather than to a financial institution. That may be true. It is perfectly compatible with the Expressibility Principle, which simply requires that any disambiguation possible at the level of

---

[1] There are important questions about what exactly it means for a thought to be linguistically expressible. Must it be expressible in an actual language? In a conceivable extension of a natural language? In a formal language, or extension thereof? Does the thinker have to be a speaker of that language? Or is it enough that there be a speaker? Or that there could be one? None of these questions will be critical for the project in this book, however. The "I"-thoughts we will primarily be looking at have fairly straightforward linguistic expressions.

[2] David Lewis, for example, has argued that there are. See Lewis 1986, §2.3.

"I": An Essential Indexical ~ 3

thought be linguistically expressible. In contrast, it might be true that thoughts are ineliminably context-sensitive.[3] There would be no conflict with Expressibility here either, even if it turned out to be the case that ineliminable context-sensitivity at the level of thought could be linguistically disambiguated.

Why should we accept the Expressibility Principle? My argument for it is very simple: Show me a counterexample. The Expressibility Principle has the commendable property of being confirmed by any attempt to refute it. In order to refute the Expressibility Principle one would have to produce an example of a thinkable but linguistically inexpressible thought. But to produce such an example is to express it. The claim here is not a trivial claim about communicability. It is obvious that a counterexample could not be communicated without being expressed, but for that very reason it would be question-begging to require that a counterexample be communicated. My point, rather, is that we have no criterion for thinkability besides linguistic expressibility.

To motivate the basic idea, consider a tip-of-the-tongue situation. You find yourself struggling to articulate something and then suddenly find the words. You say, and you may be right, that what you have done is find the words to express what you had been thinking all along. That would be fine, and perfectly compatible with the Expressibility Principle. But now imagine the same situation, but one where you don't find the words—all you have is the struggle. Would you be so confident that there was thinking going on? Now finally consider Wittgenstein's rhetorical question in *Philosophical Investigations*: "Ask yourself: 'What would it be like if human beings *never* found the word that was on the tip of their tongue?'"[4] Here it is hard to see the grounds one could have for thinking that these are episodes of thinking at all.

---

[3] As Charles Travis has repeatedly argued. See, for example, Travis 2000.
[4] Wittgenstein 1953, p. 219.

Intuitions are not arguments, however. To motivate the claim that linguistic expressibility is the criterion for thinkability we need to put the key notion of linguistic (in)expressibility on a firmer footing. Adrian Moore characterizes what it is for something non-linguistic to be linguistically expressed as follows.

x expresses y if and only if (i) x is a linguistic item with content that makes it either true or false, (ii) y is a non-linguistic item with content that makes it either true or false, and (iii) the content of x entails the content of y.[5]

For a thought to be thinkable is just for it to have truth-evaluable content. So, on this characterization, a thought that is thinkable but inexpressible would have to be a thought with a truth-evaluable content that is not entailed by the content of any linguistic item.

In this formulation, the question of what criteria there might be for holding a thought to be thinkable becomes the question of what criteria there might be for holding a thought to be evaluable for truth or falsity. Thinkability is hostage to truth evaluability. So what are the criteria for truth evaluability? We need to look at the basic properties of truth. Perhaps the most basic property is given by the disquotational schema.[6] Formulated for sentences the disquotational schema is:

The sentence "p" is true if and only if p.

As the schema brings out, sentences typically yield their own truth conditions (modulo familiar problems with indexicals and other context-sensitive expressions—to which we will of course be returning later). The left-hand side of the schema names the sentence. The right-hand side uses it to give the condition in which the named sentence is true. The schema is described as disquotational because

---

[5] Moore 2003, p. 173.
[6] See Wright 1992, chs 1 and 2 for discussion of minimal platitudes about truth, of which disquotation is one. Heck 2005 argues, in contrast, that the word "true" in English is not (and cannot be) disquotational.

the same expression appears on both sides, quoted on the left and disquoted on the right.

We can also give a disquotational schema for thoughts. One familiar device would be to use angle brackets as "quotes" for thoughts to give:

The thought $<p>$ is true if and only if p

But the most natural (and probably the only) way to interpret the expression "The thought $<p>$" is as equivalent to "The thought that p" where "p" gives the content of the thought. What else could "p" be doing inside the angle brackets other than expressing the content of the thought? This is certainly the only interpretation that allows the schema to count as a disquotational schema. But of course it requires the content of the thought to be linguistically expressible.

So, back to the original question—what are the criteria for a thought being thinkable? A minimal condition must be that a thinkable thought have a truth-evaluable content that permits disquotation. But then it is clear why any thinkable thought must be expressible. Disquotation yields the statement of a truth condition. That statement is given by the sentence on the right side of the disquotational schema. But then, to return to the characterization of (in)expressibility, the content of the sentence that states the truth condition must be identical to (and therefore entail) the content of the thought that is named/quoted on the left-hand side of the disquotation schema. And so that makes the thought linguistically expressible, by the earlier characterization of expressibility.

Certainly, this argument hinges on the claim that a thought can only be thinkable if it is subject to the disquotational schema. But that brings us back to the issue about criteria for thinkability. Thinkability requires truth evaluability. But how can one recognize that something is truth-evaluable except by understanding the condition for it to be true? And how can one understand the condition for something to be true except as linguistically expressed through the operation of disquotation? The Expressibility Principle, therefore, is grounded in the inextricable ties between thinkability, truth evaluability, and disquotation.

1.2. "I" in Language and Thought

The Expressibility Principle is a powerful methodological tool. It suggests an equivalence between thoughts and the meanings of sentences that express them. And that, in turn, suggests an equivalence between grasping a thought and understanding the sentence that expresses it. Chapter 2 offers a more detailed account of these two equivalences. For the moment we need only note the specific application that will guide the main part of this book, viz. the equivalence between entertaining "I"-thoughts and understanding "I"-sentences. Or, more precisely, the equivalence between the (conceptual) abilities exploited in entertaining "I"-thoughts and those exploited in understanding "I"-sentences.

The guiding principle for this book is that, when we have a fully self-conscious subject who is a competent user of the first person pronoun, there is a single set of abilities at the root of both their self-conscious thinking and their self-referential language. The book aims to explain what those abilities are—in particular, the role played by the mechanism of self-reference. First, though, we need to describe in more detail the phenomenon that we are trying to capture and elucidate.

In one sense "I" is a very simple linguistic device. It is an indexical expression (one whose reference varies according to the context of utterance) with a straightforward grammatical role. In English "I" is the first person singular pronoun that speakers use to refer to themselves in the role of subject. Typically in English the first person pronoun is always used when speakers refer to themselves directly— either "I," when they want to refer to themselves in the subject role, or "me," when they want to refer to themselves in the object role.

Not all languages use the first person pronoun in this way. There are *null-subject languages*, in which sentences (or more accurately, independent clauses) can grammatically lack a subject. Such languages allow the first person pronoun to be omitted. Latin is an example. Perhaps the most famous first person statement in the history of philosophy is Descartes' *"Cogito ergo sum,"* in which (ironically) the first person pronoun does not make an appearance. However, the conjugation of a Latin verb makes clear when it is being used in a way that would require it to be translated into English using "I." Latin and, to my best of my knowledge, every other human language, has devices to do the job that in English is done by "I," although some tend to leave more to context than others.

But what is that job? Sentences involving "I" have two basic features. They are:

- *Intentionally self-reflexive.* Their subject is the utterer, and this is so non-accidentally as a function of the speaker's understanding of the linguistic device.
- *Intentionally self-ascriptive.* They manifest and exploit the speaker's intention to communicate information that she knows to be about herself or to express what she herself is feeling, planning, wanting, etc.

That these are two different properties emerges from a famous thought experiment offered by Elizabeth Anscombe.

Imagine a society in which everyone is labeled with two names. One appears on their backs, and at the top of their chests, and these names, which their bearers cannot see, are various: "B" to "Z," let us say. The other, "A" is stamped on the inside of their wrists and is the same for everyone. In making reports on other people's actions everyone uses the names on their chests or backs if he can see these names and is used to seeing them. Everyone also learns to respond to utterances of the name on his or her own chest and back in the same sort of way and circumstances in which we tend to respond to utterances of our names. Reports on one's own actions, which one gives straight off from observation, are made using the name on the wrist. Such reports are made, not on the basis of observation alone, but also on that of inference and testimony or other information. *B*, for example, derives conclusions expressed by sentences with "A" as subject, from other people's statements using "B" as subject.[7]

The pronoun "A" certainly functions as an intentionally self-reflexive device. "A"-sentences are about the speaker, and non-accidentally so, as a function of the speaker's understanding of how "A" works. But the scenario is set up so that "A" is not functioning as a device of intentional self-ascription. The "A"-users are thinking of themselves third personally rather than first personally. The point of the scenario is that for each "A"-user "A" is substituting for their proper name, rather than functioning as a device to express self-conscious thoughts. Nothing significant would be lost if, instead of using "A" to refer to himself, *B* used "B." This is because *B* is not using "A" intentionally to communicate facts that he knows to be about himself. He is using "A" to communicate facts that he knows to be about *B*, but without the self-awareness that would come with knowing that he himself is *B*.

Speakers can certainly talk about themselves self-reflexively and self-ascriptively without using the first person pronoun. In fact they can even do so intentionally. Here is a nice example from Act II, Scene ii of *Julius Caesar*, when Caesar has just been warned by the augurers not to go to the Senate:

Caesar   The Gods do this in shame of cowardice:
Caesar should be a beast without a heart,
If he should stay at home for fear.
No, Caesar shall not. Danger knows full well
That Caesar is more dangerous than he:
We are two lions litter'd in one day,
And I the elder and more terrible:
And Caesar shall go forth.

[7] Anscombe 1975, p. 49.

Caesar is speaking of himself in the third person (with a brief lapse in the penultimate line). But this would hardly make sense to Calpurnia, Caesar's wife, if she were not well aware not just that Caesar was referring to himself with the name "Caesar" but also that he was doing so intentionally. So, in essence, "Caesar" here is functioning just as "I" does. In the right context a proper name can be coopted as a device of intentional self-reflexivity and self-ascription.

Remaining in the ancient world, we can contrast Caesar's intentionally self-referential use of his own name with the example of the Lydian King Croesus, as reported in the first book of Herodotus's *Histories*. Contemplating invading Persia, Croesus consults the oracle at Delphi. The oracle tells him that, should he attack the Cyrus the Great of Persia, "he would destroy a great empire."[8] Croesus fails to realize that the doomed great Empire is in fact his own. One can imagine him reporting the prophecy, referring to himself without realizing that he is referring to himself (perhaps as "A great Emperor will be defeated").

Caesar and Croesus both encounter warnings of disaster. Caesar knows that the warning is directed at him and decides to defy it. When Caesar makes his decision known he is thinking of himself and doing so self-consciously. Croesus, on the other hand, is thinking of himself, but not self-consciously. Unlike Caesar, Croesus does not realize that he himself is the subject of the prophecy. Caesar ignores the warnings of disaster knowingly. Croesus does so from ignorance.

After his defeat by Cyrus Croesus's life is spared and he sends another message to the oracle to find out what went wrong. The oracle tells him that he should have asked whether it was his empire or Cyrus's that would be destroyed. So, suppose he had done that before rather than after the fall of Sardis. He would have learnt something that he could have expressed in the sentence

---

[8] Herodotus, *Histories* 1.53. Translated by Andrea Purves in Strassler 2009.

"I am the great Emperor who will be defeated." Assuming that Croesus was more prudent than Caesar, this realization would have led him to act very differently.

A final example. In Sophocles's *Oedipus Rex* Oedipus vows to avenge the murder of Laius. He finally realizes that he himself is both Laius's murderer and Laius's son (as well as being the son, not just of Laius, but also of Jocasta, whom he subsequently and incestuously married). This realization is memorably described in his cry of despair.

> *Oedipus*   Oh god
> all come true, all burst to light!
> O light—now let me look my last on you!
> I stand revealed at last—
> cursed in my birth, cursed in marriage,
> cursed in the lives I cut down with these hands.[9]

Again, what he has realized is that he himself is the murderer of Laius; the son of Laius; and the husband of his own mother.

Many philosophers have noticed the phenomenon of intentional self-reference illustrated in these examples and remarked that there is a certain class of beliefs that have distinctive and immediate implications for action. These are beliefs with contents that can only be expressed using "I"—what John Perry famously termed *essentially indexical* beliefs.[10] Thanks to Perry and others, there are two closely related theses in broad circulation—one about agency and one about explanation:

ESSENTIAL INDEXICALITY (AGENCY)

An agent will not typically act upon beliefs about herself unless she knows, through some thought that can only be

---

[9] Sophocles, *Oedipus Rex*, ll. 1306–10. Translated by Robert Fagles in Fagles 1982.
[10] The phrase "essential indexical" is due to John Perry. See Perry 1979 and the other essays collected in Perry 1993, particularly Perry 1977. The basic phenomenon was noted, and discussed, by inter alia Castañeda 1966, 1969/1994; Anscombe 1975; and Lewis 1979.

expressed using "I," that she herself is the person those beliefs are about.

ESSENTIAL INDEXICALITY (EXPLANATION)
When explaining an action in terms of the agent's beliefs about herself, at least one of those beliefs must have as its content an "I"-thought, viz. a thought that can only be expressed using "I."

Here is a preliminary gloss. "I"-thoughts are fundamental in motivating agents and explaining action because they integrate the agent's beliefs about the world with her own first person perspective on the world. Caesar's self-referring use of his own name needs to be read as a displaced use of "I" because the thoughts that he expresses with "Caesar" display precisely this kind of integration. Caesar knows that the person to whom the prophecy has been directed is the person contemplating whether or not to go to the Senate, namely, he himself. But this integration is missing for both Croesus and Oedipus. They each have information about the world (that a great empire will be destroyed, and that the killer of Laius is still at large), but this information is not yet integrated with their own perspective on the world. So they cannot act upon it.

I proposed earlier that when we have a fully self-conscious subject competently using the first person pronoun, there is a single set of abilities at the root of both their self-conscious thinking and their self-referential language. A natural suggestion, then, would be that "I" is the linguistic manifestation of the agent's ability to integrate beliefs about the world with her own first person perspective on the world. If that is right, then explaining what it is to be able to use "I" with understanding is a way of studying that integrative ability.

1.3. The Ineliminability of "I"

The general idea of essential indexicality is close to philosophical orthodoxy. But, as Herman Cappelen and Josh Dever have pointed out in their recent book *The Inessential Indexical*, claims of essential indexicality are often driven by intuitions and examples rather than supported by arguments. (The discussion in the last section is no exception!) In this final section of this chapter I show that essential indexicals really are essential.

I will work within Cappelen and Dever's own framework. They focus on explaining action, starting with two sample action explanations.[11] One contains a putatively essential indexical. The other does not.

Personal Action Explanation
- *Belief*: François is about to be shot
- *Belief*: I am François
- *Belief (inferred)*: I am about to be shot
- *Desire*: I not be shot
- *Belief*: If I duck under the table, I will not be shot
- *Action*: I duck under the table

Impersonal Action Explanation
- *Belief*: François is about to be shot
- *Desire*: François not be shot
- *Belief*: If François ducks under the table, François will not be shot
- *Action*: François ducks under the table

The claim that they think has not yet been adequately supported is:

IIC (Impersonal Incompleteness Claim)
Impersonal action explanations are necessarily incomplete because of a missing indexical component.[12]

This is equivalent to Essential Indexicality (Explanation).

Cappelen and Dever have the following to say about the literature.

---

[11] Cappelen and Dever 2013, p. 36. They talk about rationalizations rather than explanations. I have adjusted their terminology for consistency with my own.

[12] Cappelen and Dever 2013, p. 37.

Perry's cases have the form of thought experiments in which it is *stipulated* that at t_1 there is no action (and no relevant first-person or other indexical attitude) and then at t_2 there's action. By stipulation, the only difference between t_1 and t_2 is the addition of a first-person state. So we all say: fine, yes, that could happen—the first person state could have that effect and so could play an important role in rationalization of that particular action. Note that this is at best super-weak inductive support for a strong thesis such as IIC. Without further argument, this won't justify a necessity claim like IIC. *That an ignorance of the kind the agent starts out with in Perry's examples can block rationalization of agency doesn't show that it has to.* Cases can be used as counterexamples to universal claims but can't be used to (deductively) establish the latter."[13]

I do not think that this is very fair to Perry.[14] But in any event there follows an argument on Cappelen and Dever's own terms, using their vocabulary and framing, to show that essential indexicals really are essential.

Here are three assumptions. They really just make explicit key features of Cappelen and Dever's model explanations.

Assumption 1
We explain actions by giving an idealized reconstruction of practical reasoning that the agent either did or could have gone through.

Assumption 2
An impersonal explanation reconstructs the agent's practical reasoning in terms of a set *of propositional attitudes, all of which are impersonal*.

---

[13] Ibid., pp. 41–2.
[14] There are plenty of arguments and analyses in Perry's writings on the subject, in addition to his well-known and striking examples. I offer this paper as an addition to the case already made, not as a replacement.

Assumption 3
An impersonal propositional attitude is one that refers to the agent nonindexically—for example, through a proper name or nonindexical definite description.

Moving on to the argument itself, here are three premises.

Premise 1
No explanation can correctly reconstruct an agent's practical reasoning if it is possible for that agent to hold every propositional attitude in the set and not perform the action.

Premise 2
Even if an agent holds every propositional attitude in an impersonal explanation, she will not perform the consequent action if she believes that she is not the person referred to in the explanation.

Premise 3
For any impersonal explanation it is possible for an agent to hold every propositional attitude in the set and nonetheless believe that she herself is not the person referred to in those attitudes.

Premise 1 states that the propositional attitudes in an explanation must necessitate the ensuing action. It is supported by the connection between explanation and practical reasoning highlighted in Assumption 1.

Premise 2 is not begging the question. The claim of essential indexicality is, roughly, that an agent will not perform an action unless she believes that she herself is the person referred to in the action rationalization. But Premise 2 does not make that claim. What it says is that an agent will not perform an action if she believes that she is *not* the person referred to by the attitudes in the action rationalization. So, in Impersonal Action Explanation, Premise 2 says that the agent will not duck under the table if she believes that she is not François. This seems hard to dispute.

"I": An Essential Indexical ~ 15

Premise 3 is supported by Assumptions 2 and 3. One of the key contributions of Perry's work in this area is, in effect, giving a recipe for constructing from any impersonal explanation a scenario in which an agent holds all the relevant propositional attitudes while believing that they do not apply to her.

Premises 1, 2, and 3 jointly give the incompleteness of any impersonal explanation. So we are half way there. We have:

IICa [from premises 1, 2, and 3]
Impersonal explanations are necessarily incomplete

But we haven't established that what impersonal explanations lack is an indexical (first person) component, which (by Assumption 2) would transform it into a personal explanation.

According to Assumption 3 any impersonal explanation refers to the agent nonindexically—for example, through a proper name or nonindexical definite description. Let "φ" stand for however the agent is referred to. There are two ways in which the incompleteness identified in IICa could be remedied. We could require that an impersonal explanation satisfy one or other of the following two conditions.

Condition 1
The agent must believe that she herself is φ.
Condition 2
The agent must not believe that she herself is not φ.

Condition 1 gives us essential indexicality, because it states that what is missing in impersonal explanations is a specific indexical belief—which, by Assumption 3, would transform the explanation into a personal one.

Condition 2, in contrast, says that what is missing is not a specific belief, but simply the absence of the problematic belief that she (the agent) is not herself φ. An opponent of essential indexicality might say that this is simply a background assumption of any impersonal explanation. For example, it is implicit in the sample explanation given earlier that the agent should not believe that he himself is not François.

It is not hard to show that Condition 2 fails to motivate action in some scenarios. As before, let "φ" be a description or proper name referring to the agent in an impersonal explanation. Suppose that the agent is in the process of trying to find out whether or not she is φ. *Ex hypothesi* she neither believes that she is φ nor believes that she is not φ. So Condition 2 is satisfied. Suppose also that she knows there is something that the person who is φ should do (if "φ" is "the winner of the raffle" then this might be going to collect the prize, for example). Surely her state of uncertainty as to whether she is φ or not precludes her acting on propositional attitudes concerning φ, even though she is φ.

But, Cappelen and Dever are likely to ask, how can one get a universal thesis out of this? The fact that Condition 2 is not sufficient to motivate action certainly doesn't entail that Option 1 is necessary.

But it does show that we need to extend the implicit Condition 2 on the impersonal account as follows:

Condition 2*
The agent (a) must not believe that she herself is not φ, and (b) must not be uncertain as to whether or not she herself is φ

But now think about an agent satisfying Condition 2*. What would it be for an agent neither to believe that she is not φ nor to be uncertain as to whether or not she is φ? The defender of impersonal explanation confronts a dilemma.

Here is the first horn. Obviously one way in which an agent might satisfy Condition 2* would be by believing that she herself is φ. But of course that would collapse Condition 2* into Condition 1, since the belief that she herself is φ is an indexical belief.

So how might an agent satisfy Condition 2* without satisfying Condition 1? How should we think about the psychology of an agent of whom the following things are all true?

"I": An Essential Indexical ~ 17

(i) She does not believe that she herself is φ
(ii) She does not believe that she herself is not φ
(iii) She is not uncertain as to whether or not she is φ.

The only way that I can see in which an agent might simultaneously satisfy (i) through (iii) is if it has never occurred to her whether or not she might be φ.

This gives us the second horn of the dilemma. If it has never occurred to me that I might be φ then why would I act upon a set of propositional attitudes conceptualized in terms of φ? If it has never occurred to me that I might have won the raffle, why would I go to collect the prize? There is certainly no danger of conceding the point to the essential indexicality theorist (as on the first horn). But the price to be paid is that the impersonal propositional attitudes cannot motivate the agent.

This dilemma shows that Condition 2* cannot be the right way of resolving the incompleteness of impersonal explanations identified in IICa. But Condition 1 and Condition 2* are mutually exhaustive. What we have seen in effect is that the only way in which Condition 1 could fail to hold (and action be motivated) is if Condition 2* holds, and vice versa.

So we have to revert to Condition 1, which requires adequate explanations to include an "I"-thought that "anchors" the impersonal propositional attitudes to the agent's first person perspective.

Adding Condition 1 to IICa essentially gives us

ESSENTIAL INDEXICALITY (EXPLANATION)
When explaining an action in terms of the agent's beliefs about herself, at least one of those beliefs must have as its content an "I"-thought, viz. a thought that can only be expressed using "I."

Moreover, since the entire argument has exploited the reciprocal relationship between how actions are motivated and how actions are explained, we also have

ESSENTIAL INDEXICALITY (AGENCY)
An agent will not typically act upon beliefs about herself unless she knows, through some thought that can only be expressed using "I," that she herself is the person those beliefs are about.

1.4. Summary

The starting point for exploring the first person in language and thought is the Expressibility Principle, according to which any thinkable thought can be linguistically expressed without residue or remainder. This principle suggests an equivalence between grasping a thought and understanding the sentence that expresses it—and, in particular, between entertaining "I"-thoughts and understanding "I"-sentences. Extending this further, the guiding principle for this book is that, for fully self-conscious subject who are competent users of the first person pronoun, a single set of abilities underlies both self-conscious thinking and self-referential language.

To begin elucidating those abilities we started with two basic features of "I"-sentences. They are *intentionally self-reflexive* and *intentionally self-ascriptive*. Exploring those two properties led to two theses about the indispensable role of "I"-thoughts in motivating and explaining action. The *essential indexicality* thesis about action is that agents will typically not act upon beliefs unless those beliefs are anchored to themselves through "I"-thoughts. The correlative belief about explanation is that adequately explaining action requires specifying an anchoring "I"-thought. I gave an argument to show that these anchoring "I"-thoughts really are essential. They make it possible for an agent to integrate her beliefs about the world with her own first person perspective on the world.

2

Sense and Understanding

Chapter 1 established two theses affirming the importance of "I"-thoughts in motivating and explaining action:

ESSENTIAL INDEXICALITY (AGENCY)
An agent will not typically act upon beliefs about herself unless she knows, through some thought that can only be expressed using "I," that she herself is the person those beliefs are about.

ESSENTIAL INDEXICALITY (EXPLANATION)
When explaining an action in terms of the agent's beliefs about herself, at least one of those beliefs must have as its content an "I"-thought, viz. a thought that can only be expressed using "I."

The task for this book is to give a full account of "I"-thoughts—how they are structured; how they work; and what they contribute to the mental lives of self-conscious agents.

From a methodological point of view, the Expressibility Principle suggests that we can give an account of "I"-thoughts through thinking about what is involved in using and understanding "I"-sentences. Plainly, therefore, we need a general framework for thinking about linguistic understanding. The framework that I will propose is based on Frege's notion of sense.

Unfortunately, Frege's notion of sense has taken something of a battering in recent years. Here is a representative passage from Jeffrey King:

Thoughts are supposed to be composed of the senses of names, predicates, and so on. And the main motivation for thinking these expressions have senses, given in "On Sinn and Bedeutung", is that names need to be assigned senses to account for certain features of identity sentences. Of course, Donnellan, Kripke, and their followers have given strong reasons for thinking that names don't have senses. But then such arguments undercut the motivation for senses generally. Hence we have been give good reason to think that the alleged component parts of thought do not exist.[1]

King is expressing a widely held view. Frege's notion of sense is out of fashion as a tool for understanding language. For some aspects of Frege's view this may be justified. It seems to me, however, that the discussion has focused on a narrow range of topics (particularly, natural language identity sentences and belief reports) to the exclusion of broader areas where Frege's contribution is potentially more enduring.

Section 2.1 presents the standard picture of Frege's approach to language and and how it contrasts with direct reference approaches. Section 2.2 argues that the notion of sense is best taken as an account of linguistic understanding, and when so taken it is perfectly compatible with the direct reference view to which it is standardly opposed. In section 2.3 I explore the general connections between understanding and truth, before turning in section 2.4 to what it is to understand proper names.

2.1. *The Standard Contrast: Frege vs. Russell*

Textbooks and survey articles in the philosophy of language typically contrast two approaches to the meaning of sentences (and hence the content of the thoughts that they express). One has its roots in Frege. The other is attributed variously to Mill and/or

[1] King 2007, pp. 18–19.

Russell. According to Robert Stalnaker, for example, the two approaches offer radically different answers to the descriptive-semantic question: What kind of thing can be the semantic value of a proper name? Stalnaker defines a semantic value as follows:

> The term "semantic value," as I am using it, is a general and neutral term for whatever it is that a semantic theory associates with the expressions of the language it interprets; the things that, according to the semantics, provide the interpretations of simple expressions, and are the arguments and values of the functions defined by the compositional rules that interpret the complex expressions.[2]

He then sketches out what he takes to be the Millian and Fregean responses to this question.

> Kripke's answer to the first question—the descriptive-semantic question about proper names—is the Millian answer; the semantic value of a name is simply its referent. The contrasting answer that he argued against [viz. the Fregean answer] is that the semantic value of a name is a general concept that mediates between a name and its referent: a concept of the kind that might be expressed by a definite description. According to this contrasting answer, the semantic value of the name—its sense or connotation—determines a referent for the name as a function of the facts; the referent, if there is one, is the unique individual that fits the concept, or perhaps the individual that best fits the concept.[3]

Stalnaker attributes the following theses to supporters of Frege: that the semantic value of a proper name is not its referent; that the semantic value of a proper name is a general concept; and that the semantic value of a proper name determines its referent. In opposition to all this the Russell/Mill view is supposed to maintain simply that the semantic value of a proper name is the object that it names, its bearer.[4]

---

[2] Stalnaker 1997, p. 535.   [3] Ibid. p. 536.
[4] The original modern proponent of the Russell/Mill view appears to have been Ruth Barcan Marcus. See her 1961.

It will be helpful for the following to represent these two models diagrammatically. I will show how each of them is supposed to analyze my utterance of the sentence "I am F." Figure 2.1 depicts the model identified as Frege's.

On this model, when I utter the sentence "I am F," the utterance expresses a thought, which is composed of senses—the sense of the expression "I" (designated by "•I•," using Sellars's device of dot-quotation) and the sense of the expression "– is F" (designated by "•–is F•"). The distinct senses in the thought pick out an object and a property respectively. So, "•I•" determines myself, JLB, as the semantic value of "I," while "•– is F•" determines the

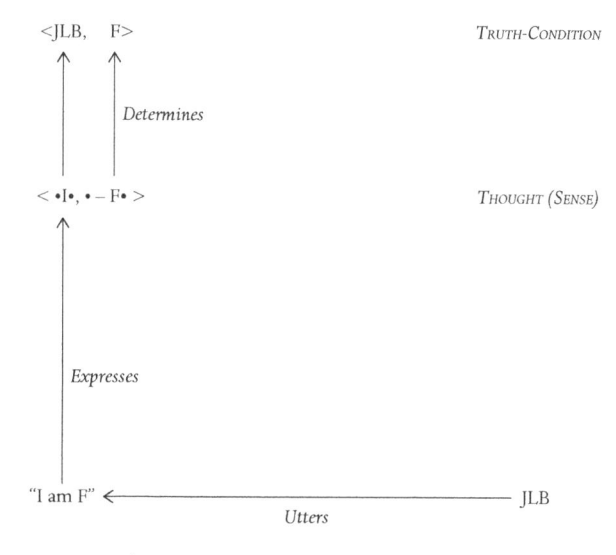

```
<JLB,   F>                              TRUTH-CONDITION
  ↑    ↑
  |    |
  |    | Determines
  |    |
< •I•, • – F• >                         THOUGHT (SENSE)
  ↑
  |
  |
  |
  |
  | Expresses
  |
  |
"I am F"  ←─────────────────────────── JLB
                    Utters
```

Figure 2.1 A schematic representation of how my utterance of the sentence "I am F" would be interpreted on a Fregean model of language, as standardly understood in contemporary philosophy of language. I am using Sellar's dot-quotation device to designate sense, so that "•I•" designated the sense of the first person pronoun "I." Angle brackets designate composition, however that is achieved. See the text for further explanation.

Sense and Understanding ~ 23

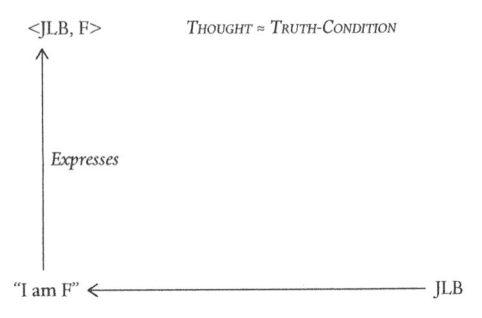

```
    <JLB, F>            THOUGHT ≈ TRUTH-CONDITION
       ↑
       |
       |
     Expresses
       |
       |
       |
    "I am F" ←————————————————————— JLB
```

Figure 2.2 A schematic representation of how my utterance of the sentence "I am F" would be interpreted on the Russell/Mill model of language, as standardly understood in contemporary philosophy of language. Angle brackets designate composition, however that is achieved.

property F.[5] This gives the truth condition of the sentence: As uttered by JLB, "I am F" is true if and only if JLB is F. (I am using angled brackets to designate composition, however that composition is achieved.)

Compare this model with the Russell/Mill model depicted in Figure 2.2. Here there is no intervening level of sense. The content of the thought is directly given by the utterance's truth condition.

Given the simplicity of the Russell/Mill model it is unsurprising that philosophers have taken a hard look at the much more complex and cumbersome Fregean model. Discussion has focused in particular on two puzzles standardly taken to have motivated the historical Frege. The first is the puzzle of explaining how identity sentences can be informative. The second is the problem of explaining the semantics of belief ascriptions. It is fair to say,

---

[5] This is not really true to Frege, for whom predicates refer to concepts, which are functions. But nothing in the following will be lost by making this aspect of the Fregean position consist with the Russell/Mill position. For more on Frege's views here see Oliver 2010 and Ricketts 2010.

I think, that the majority of philosophers of language and thought are unconvinced that solving either of these problems requires Frege's notion of sense.

This is hardly surprising, however. Unless the notion of sense were independently motivated, why would one think that it could provide a satisfactory solution to problems about informative identities or belief ascriptions? And, conversely, why would it make sense to base an entire semantic theory on a proposed solution to problems in very circumscribed areas of language?[6]

It does not help that the dominant interpretation of senses in terms of definite descriptions is at odds in many ways with how we use language and understand proper names. Names still succeed in referring even when the user of the name has wildly incorrect beliefs about the referent. And proper names often behave very differently in modal contexts from definite descriptions. Both of these points were powerfully made by Kripke and still command widespread assent.[7]

For these reasons the rejection of Fregean sense seems reasonable within the standard framework of discussion. If you think that the notion of sense is motivated solely by puzzles about informative identities and belief ascriptions, and you think that the senses of proper names are best understood as definite descriptions that fix the referents of the names as the individuals that best satisfy the descriptions, then you would be well advised to be skeptical of the notion. But it seems to me that we need take another look at the standard framework.

---

[6] It is true that, from Frege's perspective, the problem of informative identities was hardly circumscribed, given that he was interested primarily in mathematics, rather than natural language, and mathematics is the science of informative identity statements. But this aspect of Frege's thought is rarely if ever brought into the picture in philosophical discussions of sense.

[7] Key texts are Kripke 1980; Donnellan 1966; and Kaplan 1989.

2.2. Why Do We Need a Notion of Sense?

Frege's notion of sense is better seen as answering a much broader question about language than the nature of informative identities and the semantics of belief ascriptions.[8] Frege's sharp distinction between the level of sense and the level of reference carves out an explanatory space for tackling the fundamental question of what it is to understand language. The level of reference is the level of truth, while the level of sense is the level of understanding. The basic insight driving the theory of sense as a theory of understanding is the equation between understanding a sentence and grasping the thought that it expresses, which is equated in turn with knowing the conditions under which the sentence counts as true. These two equations allow us to develop a Fregean account of understanding that is orthogonal to the standard contrast between Frege, on the one hand, and Russell/Mill on the other.

So, to answer the question in the title of the section, we need a notion of sense because we need an account of understanding. The sense of an expression, whether that expression is a proper name, a logical constant, a predicate or a complete sentence, is what a competent language-user understands when he understands that expression.[9] The Fregean model of sense and understanding takes understanding a complete sentence to be basic, because it takes the notion of truth to be fundamental to understanding and truth is a property of sentences and the thoughts that they express.

---

[8] I am not offering the following as a contribution to Frege exegesis. It will be obvious that what I say about Frege's notion of sense is deeply influenced by Michael Dummett, particularly in Dummett 1973, chs 5 and 6; Gareth Evans (1982); Tyler Burge (particularly 1979 and 1990); and Kremer 2010.

[9] As Burge points out, Frege often seems to be talking about something much more idealized than a highly competent language-user, allowing that even highly competent language-users can grasp senses imperfectly (Burge 1990). Certainly understanding comes in degrees and is deeply normative. And I agree with Burge that Frege's notion of sense is not best viewed as an account of conventional linguistic meaning (but as will emerge in later chapters) the notion of understanding is far richer than the notion of conventional linguistic meaning.

Grasping a complete thought (the sense of a sentence) is a way of apprehending a sentence's truth-condition—a way of apprehending how the world would have to be for the sentence to be true. The senses of sub-sentential expressions are given in terms of apprehending the individual constituents of the truth condition (the semantic values of the sub-sentential expressions) and how they contribute to the truth condition of the sentence a whole.

These rudimentary thoughts about truth and understanding are hardly controversial. In fact they seem platitudinous. That is the intention. If grasping the sense of a sentence just is apprehending its truth condition, then it is hard to see why anyone would think that we can dispense with the notion of sense. The rub comes, of course, with how the relationship between sense and truth-condition is understood—in particular, with how, for sub-sentential expressions, the relation between sense and semantic value is understood.

In Figure 2.1 the relation between sense and truth condition is diagrammed in terms of determination. One relatively innocuous way of interpreting Frege's dictum that sense determines reference would be as holding that it is not possible for two expressions with the same sense to have different referents. Within the standard framework, however, it is usual to interpret determination more strongly. The passage from Stalnaker quoted earlier is a good example.

[T]he semantic value of the name—its sense or connotation—determines a referent for the name as a function of the facts; the referent, if there is one, is the unique individual that fits the concept, or perhaps the individual that best fits the concept.[10]

Particularly when applied to proper names in natural language, this way of thinking about sense leads to the difficulties identified by Kripke, Kaplan, and others. Language just doesn't seem to work that way. Proper names and general concepts (such as definite

---

[10] Ibid. p. 536.

Sense and Understanding ~ 27

descriptions) behave very differently from each other, particularly (but not exclusively) in modal contexts.

Do we have to think about sense in the way Stalnaker suggests? It is true that Frege's examples of the senses of proper names often take the form of definite descriptions, but it is not really clear what Frege thought about the senses of proper names—or even whether he had a settled position. His writings do, though, contain hints and suggestions that point toward a very different way of thinking about how sense relates to reference.

An alternative approach to Frege's idea of sense emphasizes its role as a mode of presentation of the entities that are semantic values of linguistic expressions. Tyler Burge sees this as a fundamental dimension, perhaps the fundamental dimension, of Frege's thinking about sense.

> Senses are "modes of presentation": ways things are presented to a thinker—or ways a thinker conceives of or otherwise represents entities in those cases where there are no entities. Not all modes of presentation are senses. But where modes of presentation are senses, they are associated with linguistic expressions. Being a sense is not essential to the entities that are senses. Being a (possible) mode of presentation to a thinker is what is fundamental. A sense is a mode of presentation that is "grasped" by those "sufficiently familiar" with the language to which an expression belongs.[11]

This idea of a mode of presentation is not just intended to apply to proper names. Thoughts are modes of presentation, as are the senses of other sub-sentential expressions besides names. What entities do thoughts present? Frege's official view is that thought are modes of presentation of truth values—true thoughts present the True and false thoughts the False—but Kremer presents a convincing case that Frege allowed truth values to have parts

---

[11] Burge 1990 at pp. 242–3 in the reprint in Burge 2005.

```
     <JLB, F>                              TRUTH-CONDITION
      ↑    ↑
    Mode│ of │Presentation
     < •|•, • – F• >                       THOUGHT/SENSE
      ↑        ↖
                  Grasps
      │
      │    Expresses
      │
      │            ←────
                  Utters
     "I am F"    Understands              JLB
```

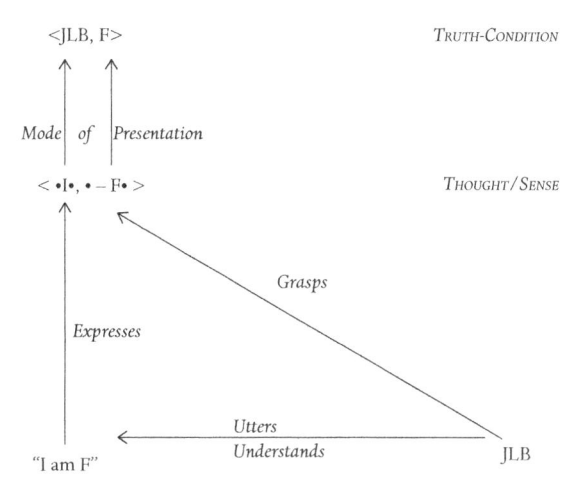

Figure 2.3 A more accurate depiction of the Fregean model of sense, incorporating the dimension of understanding and the idea that sense is a mode of presentation of reference.

corresponding to the distinct semantic values.[12] For that reason I think it would not be straining the Fregean picture too much to interpret thoughts as modes of presentation of truth conditions. The model can now be diagrammed as in Figure 2.3.

The principal changes over Figure 2.1 are replacing the idea of senses determining referents (semantic values) with the idea of senses as modes of presentation of semantic values, and making explicit the dimension of understanding.

Nothing so far ought to be unacceptable to proponents of the Russell/Mill model. I don't see how a Russell/Mill theorist could deny that a proper account of language and thought needs to incorporate an account of linguistic understanding. Their quarrel is not with the idea that we need an account of understanding, but rather with the proposal to incorporate understanding into the nature of the thought (proposition) that the sentence expresses.

---

[12] Kremer 2010, pp. 267–8.

Sense and Understanding

```
< JLB, F>        TRUTH CONDITION ≈ THOUGHT
  ↑ ↖
  |    ↖  Presents
  |       ↖
  |         < •I•, • – F• >
  |              ↖
Expresses          ↖
  |                  ↖ Grasps
  |                     ↖
  |         Utters
"I am F"  ←─────────────────  JLB
            Understands
```

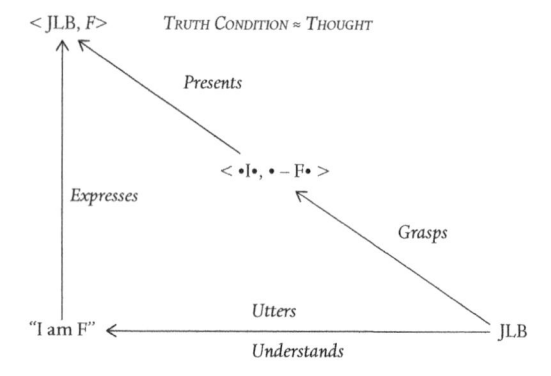

Figure 2.4 The hybrid view, which is the Russell/Mill model expanded to incorporate a Fregean account of linguistic understanding in terms of sense.

Moreover, as remarked earlier, the idea that understanding a sentence is a matter of appreciating how the world would have to be for the sentence to be true is uncontroversial to the point of platitude. So too is the idea that understanding sub-sentential expressions is a matter of understanding how their semantic values contribute to determining the truth-conditions of sentences in which they feature. So, at least given the somewhat schematic notion of sense currently in play, it certainly seems open to the Russell/Mill theorist to hold a hybrid view that might be diagrammed as in Figure 2.4.

The hybrid view leaves unchallenged the basic tenet of the Russell/Mill theory that what a sentence expresses (its content) is a Russellian proposition, composed of objects and properties. But it incorporates the Fregean notion of sense as an account of understanding.[13]

---

[13] The hybrid view is already represented in the literature. In *Frege's Puzzle*, for example, Nathan Salmon uses the notion of a propositional guise to analyze belief reports. A guise is a manner of grasping a proposition, built up from manners of grasping the constituents of the proposition (Salmon 1983). Graeme Forbes suggested in his review of the book that this comes close to a notational variant of

Theories of direct reference are typically silent on the question of what it is to understand a proper name. The question that Kripke addresses in the second lecture of *Naming and Necessity* is the rather different question of what makes it the case that a given proper name is associated with a given object as its referent.[14] The basic picture of an original baptism followed by a series of reference-preserving links might provide an answer to the question of what makes it the case that a given proper name has the semantic value that it has. But it will not tell us what it is that a competent speaker knows when he understands the name in question—what it is that distinguishes a competent user of a proper name from someone who merely picks up on a name in a passing conversation?[15] Kripke and others, impressed by the fact that a speaker who possesses little or no information about the bearer of a name can still use the name to refer to its bearer, offer a theory explaining how reference is secured on such an occasion. But, since what they are effectively explaining is how a speaker who doesn't understand a name can nonetheless use it to pick out its bearer, the theory is of necessity silent on the question of how we should characterize a speaker who *does* understand a proper name.

So, the relevant opposition is not between Frege's theory of sense and some version of the causal theory of reference. These are answers to different questions. A more appropriate alternative to the theory of sense is Russell's view that "to understand a name you must be acquainted with the particular of which it is the

---

Frege's view (Forbes 1987). Still, it is not clear that the theory of guises is being offered as a general account of linguistic understanding. Recanati 1993 takes a different hybrid approach.

[14] See, for example, Kripke 1980, p. 96. McKinsey 1984 and 2010 distinguishes the question of what sort of proposition is expressed by sentences using proper names from the question of how the referents of names are fixed. The theory of Russellian propositions answers the first question. The causal theory of reference answers the second. But neither answers the question of what it is to understand a proper name.

[15] As noted in Dummett 1973, pp. 146–51.

name."[16] Russell's principle of acquaintance addresses the same question as Frege's theory of sense, but when interpreted as Russell interpreted it the answer it offers is clearly unsatisfactory.[17] It is not hard to see why it should have led Russell to his completely unacceptable denial of the status of proper name to almost everything that we intuitively think of as a proper name. Nothing like Russell's version of the principle of acquaintance can serve as a coherent alternative to Frege's account of linguistic understanding.

In fact, to return to the causal theory of reference, it is perfectly compatible with the hybrid view to think of reference in the way that the causal theory does. There is no inconsistency in holding that the semantic values of names are fixed as the causal theory suggests, while also holding that our understanding of those names consists in our thinking of their semantic values in certain ways (under certain modes of presentation). This is because there is no requirement to interpret Frege's dictum that sense determines reference as giving an answer to the question that the causal theory of reference is intended to answer—the question of what makes it the case that *this* name picks out *that* object. As Burge points out, "Frege explicates the notion of fixing a *Bedeutung* in a purely logical way: for each sense there is at most one *Bedeutung*. It is also clear, partly from the first function [i.e. serving as a mode of presentation of the *Bedeutung*], that sense is a way of thinking of *Bedeutung*. Beyond the foregoing, Frege says little."[18]

Admittedly, if the Fregean were committed to holding, first, that all senses are really disguised definite descriptions, and second, that descriptive senses behave in modal contexts in the way that Kripke and others claim, then we would have grounds to interpret the "sense determines reference" dictum so that it would conflict with a causal theory of reference. The reason for the second

---

[16] Russell 1918, p. 205.
[17] The point is clearly and decisively made in Sainsbury 1979, pp. 26–41.
[18] Burge 1990 at p. 243 (as reprinted in his 2005). My emphasis.

qualification is that some authors have argued that descriptive senses can be understood in ways that make them immune to Kripke-type modal arguments hinging on the different behavior of proper names and definite descriptions in modal contexts.[19] But really this is beside the point. It is not promising to interpret Frege as holding that all proper names are synonymous with definite descriptions—and even less so to think that this is a requirement upon the Fregean model.[20]

As has been frequently observed, there is a crucial difference between stating the sense of a proper name and indicating it indirectly.[21] This is the *Tractatus* distinction between saying and showing. One standard way of showing the sense of a proper name is by specifying its reference. In the famous footnote about Aristotle in "On Sense and Reference" the sense of the proper name "Aristotle" is shown by identifying its referent by means of a definite description ("the pupil of Aristotle and the teacher of Alexander the Great"). But even though the sense of a proper name might be shown by picking out its referent with a definite description, it by no means follows that the definite description in question *has* the sense of the name. Here is an example. I might show the sense of the name "Fido" by picking Fido out with a definite description of the form "the first dog that I saw yesterday after lunch." This does not entail that the name "Fido" is synonymous with that definite description. And nor would that be very plausible. More plausible would be the thought that the sense

---

[19] See, for example, Dummett 1973, appendix to Chapter 5; Dummett 1981, pp. 557–601; and Burge 1979. But see Soames 1998 and, for a response, Burge 2003b.

[20] Clearly, some proper names are synonymous with definite descriptions. Examples are "Pseudo-Scotus," which picks out the author of the logical works originally attributed to Duns Scotus (there are many similar examples in the history of ancient and medieval philosophy), and "African Eve," referring to our earliest common female ancestor. There are also the descriptive names discussed in Evans 1973, such as the name "Julius," introduced as "the inventor of the zip." But it should be apparent how unusual these are.

[21] See Dummett 1973, p. 227; McDowell 1977; Bell 1979, p. 63.

Sense and Understanding

I associate with the name "Fido" is some kind of ability to recognize Fido derived from my encounter with him yesterday after lunch.

In any event, the main points for the moment are, first, that we should think of Frege's theory of sense as a theory of understanding and, second, that thought of in this way there is room in logical space for the Fregean theory (suitably developed) to complement the Russell/Mill model, as the hybrid view proposes. Section 2.3 will look more closely at how we might think about the relation between sense, understanding, and truth-conditions.

2.3. Sense, Truth-Conditions, and Understanding

The following four platitudes capture the idea that sense is correlative with understanding.

- The sense of an expression, whether that expression is a proper name, a logical constant, a predicate or a complete sentence, is what a competent language-user understands when he understands that expression.
- The notion of truth is fundamental to linguistic understanding.
- To understand a sentence is to understand its truth condition (how the world would have to be for it to be true).
- To understand sub-sentential expressions is to understand how they contribute to determining the truth-conditions of sentences in which they feature.

This section puts flesh on the bone of these platitudes, hopefully in an acceptable way both to the Fregean and to direct reference theorists.

In explaining what it is to grasp a sentence's truth condition we cannot require that the language user actually be in a position to determine whether the sentence is true or false. We do not want an account of linguistic understanding that sneaks in verificationism by the back door, making it impossible to accommodate the fact that we plainly do manage to understand sentences whose truth value there is no possibility of determining—sentences about the distant past, for example, or about the future.

But on the other hand we need an account of linguistic understanding more substantive than simply applying the disquotational principle. The disquotational schema certainly gives a way of specifying the truth condition for any truth-apt sentence. If we are given:

(*) "83 is a prime number" is true if and only if 83 is a prime number

then we are certainly given the condition for "83 is a prime number" to be true. But we are not given the sentence's truth condition in a way that we could use, for example, to explain what the sentence means to someone unfamiliar with the concept of a prime number. Someone who does not know what a prime number is can assent to (*).

So, what would a more substantive account look like? Let's start for simplicity with an atomic sentence of the form *"a is F."* As noted, someone who does not understand the sentence *"a is F"* can know that *"a is F"* is true if and only if *a* is *F*. What would such a person need to acquire in order to understand the sentence? A verificationist would say that what is missing is knowledge of a procedure for determining whether *a* is *F*. This response manages to be both too strong and too weak, however. It is too strong because we understand many sentences for which we have no inkling of a procedure for determining their truth value. The reasons for which it is too weak, though, are more subtle. Let's go back to the sentence "83 is a prime number" and let's say that I don't understand this sentence because I don't understand the expression "—is prime." Suppose that you try to help me out by teaching me a procedure for generating prime numbers. You might teach me the sieve of Eratosthenes, for example. If I know the sieve of Eratosthenes then I have a procedure for determining, for any arbitrary number, whether or not it is prime. So I certainly have a procedure for determining the truth-value of the sentence "83 is a prime number." And in fact I could apply the algorithm and discover that 83 is indeed a prime number. But, even having done all that, I still might not understand the sentence "83 is a prime number," because I might still not know that a prime number is a number divisible only by 1 and itself. I can know and apply the procedure without knowing what the procedure is trying to establish. This would be a situation where, although I have used a reliable procedure to establish that the sentence is true, I still don't know what the condition is for it to be true.

What is important for understanding a sentence is certainly not that one know how to establish that sentence's truth-value. Nor is it knowing what would count as evidence for its truth. Rather it is knowing what would count as the sentence being true—knowing which state of affairs would make it true. To understand "*a* is *F*" is to know what would count as *a* being *F*. To get further purchase on this idea, though, we need to look at how this plays out at the sub-sentential level, and so at the contributions made by the understanding of "*a*" and "– is *F*."

On the second of these, we cannot accept Dummett's proposal that understanding a predicate consists in a means of determining whether or not an object falls within the extension of the predicate for reasons that came out in the discussion of "83 is a prime number."[22] Possessing such a procedure is useful only if one knows what the intended end-point is supposed to be, which in turn requires knowing what it would be for an arbitrary object to fall under the predicate. And it is in possession of this knowledge, rather than possession of the procedure, that understanding of the predicate consists. Names are more complicated and have been more discussed. We turn to them in section 2.4.

[22] Dummett 1973, chs 5 and 6.

2.4. Understanding Names

What does one need to know about "*a*" in order to know what would count as *a* being *F*? Some authors have offered a deflationary account of what it is to understand a proper name.[23] The deflationary proposal, in brief, is that one can properly be described as understanding a proper name "*a*" if and only if one knows that "*a*" refers to *a*. To understand the proper names "J. K. Rowling" or "π" one need only know that they refer to J. K. Rowling and π respectively.

One advantage of this proposal is that it places no further requirement on understanding a proper name in a particular language over and above knowledge of the axiom in the truth theory for the relevant language that gives the semantic value of the name in question—that is, the axioms that "J. K. Rowling" stands for J. K. Rowling and that "π" stands for π. But the danger is that understanding a proper name becomes a commodity too easily acquired to be valuable. To know that "J. K. Rowling" stands for J. K. Rowling I need only know that "J. K. Rowling" is a proper name, have some reason to think that it has a bearer, and be able to perform a disquotational trick. But those pieces of knowledge are not going to help me understand sentences in which the name "J. K. Rowling" appears, because they will not help me to know what would count as J. K. Rowling having some property or other. They do not give me any kind of cognitive fix on the individual J. K. Rowling.

It is true that I would have some very minimal knowledge of J. K. Rowling. I would know, of her, that she is the bearer of the name "J. K. Rowling." Some philosophers have been sufficiently moved by this to propose thinking of proper names as, in effect, metalinguistic descriptions.[24] On this view, the proper name

---

[23] See, for example, McDowell 1977; Sainsbury 1979, pp. 82–7.
[24] See, for example, Sainsbury 1979; Bach 2002; Katz 2001; Burgess 2013.

Sense and Understanding ~ 37

"J. K. Rowling" is synonymous with the description "the bearer of the name 'J. K. Rowling'." But this still does not help me understand how the world would have to be in order for a sentence containing the name "J. K. Rowling" to be true. Knowing that "J. K. Rowling is a famous novelist" is true if and only if the bearer of the name "J. K. Rowling" is a famous novelist does not seem to me to be a significant advance upon knowing that "J. K. Rowling is a famous novelist" is true if and only if J. K. Rowling is a famous novelist.

To appreciate the reasoning behind (and the shortcomings of) both the deflationary view and the related metalinguistic view, consider the following passage from Sainsbury:

> Fido goes by; we point him out and say "that's Fido"; our audience comes to understand the name "Fido". What more has happened, relevant to this understanding, than that our audience has come to know, of Fido, that he is named "Fido"? Surely the answer is: nothing. There seems to be only one serious source of opposition to this answer. This is that, in addition, the audience has come to associate the name "Fido" with some description, a description which encapsulates the meaning of the name (or which will serve to encapsulate the meaning the name will have in the audience's idiolect). (Sainsbury 1979, p. 83)

But there is another possible answer. Clearly, the audience won't have learnt of Fido that he is named "Fido" unless they follow the ostensive gesture and actually see Fido. Perhaps what they thereby come to acquire is an ability to recognize Fido as the bearer of the name "Fido" should they run into him on another occasion. This recognitional ability may well be fallible. They might mistake a similar-looking dog for Fido in the future. But, for all that, if they don't acquire such an ability (if, for example, Fido runs by too fast) then they just won't have learnt of Fido that he is named "Fido." And, most importantly, it is absurd to equate this acquisition of a recognitional ability with the acquisition of a piece of descriptive knowledge. Only philosophical prejudice could require that every perceptually based recognitional ability should be linguistically expressible in the form of a description, and clearly (from the perspective of a Fregean theory of sense) it is the recognitional ability that is paramount.

Let's continue with the example of Fido, who happens to be a racing greyhound. As it happens, Fido races under the name "Ozymandias." One of the bystanders, already familiar with the dog and cognizant that "Ozymandias" names Ozymandias and that "Fido" names Fido, recognizes Fido at the track and learns the truth of the identity statement "Fido is Ozymandias." What has he learnt? According to the deflationary account and metalinguistic descriptivism, he has learnt the twin facts that "Fido" names Ozymandias and that "Ozymandias" names Fido. He certainly didn't know either fact already, even though he understood both names and hence knew that "Fido" names Fido and that "Ozymandias" names Ozymandias. That much must be granted. But, nonetheless, is what the bystander learns the metalinguistic fact that the two names "Ozymandias" and "Fido" refer to one and the same dog?

Frege certainly thought so early in his career in the *Begriffschrifft*, but he famously retracted at the beginning of "On Sinn and Bedeutung."

> If the sign "a" is distinguished from the sign "b" only as an object (here, by means of its shape), not as a sign (i.e. not by the manner in which it designates something), the cognitive value of a = a becomes essentially equal to that of a = b, provided a = b is true. A difference can arise only if the difference between the signs corresponds to a difference in the mode of presentation.[25]

Taken at face value this argument is not convincing. Generally, if someone knows, concerning a, that "a" names a, and it is the case

---

[25] Frege 1892, p. 151. See section 5 of Kremer 2010 for an analysis of the section of "Uber Sinn und Bedeutung" repudiating the metalinguistic view proposed in *Begriffschrifft* §8.

Sense and Understanding ~ 39

that a = b, then he knows, concerning b, that "a" names b. It doesn't follow of course that he knows that "a" names b. But a more charitable reading of Frege's misgivings with the metalinguistic account lies easily to hand. The basic problem is that what one learns when one learns the truth of an identity statement is not a fact about a particular language (namely, that two of its expressions are co-referential). Rather, it is a fact about the world, namely, that where one had previously thought that there were two objects (or had been unsure whether there was one object or two) there is really only one. The theory of sense can accommodate this because it states that what we learn in learning the truth of an identity statement is, effectively, that one and the same object can be thought about in two different ways—that we have two different ways of picking out and re-identifying one single object. The fact in question would be the same even if the actual proper names associated with these two different ways of thinking about the object were different, whereas in such a situation the metalinguistic theory would be forced to identify a different fact. The fact that "l'étoile du matin" and "l'étoile du soir" are co-referential is a different fact from the fact that "Hesperus" and "Phosphorus" are co-referential. But the two identity statements "l'étoile du matin = l'étoile du soir" and "Hesperus = Phosphorus" are both made true by the same fact—the fact that there is one object being thought of in the relevant two different ways, one associated with its being seen in the morning and the other associated with its being seen in the evening.

There are of course many different ways of thinking about objects, and correspondingly considerable variance across proper names. The descriptive model is required for names such as "African Eve" where the intention is to pick out a single person as the earliest common ancestor of living humans. For the names of other historical figures, it may be more profitable to think about their sense in terms of abilities to acquire information. Understanding the name "Aristotle" is being able to tap into multiple streams of information originating from a historical personage, so that one knows that sentences containing "Aristotle" are true just if the source of the information streams has the properties attributed by the sentence. Perceptual recognition is also important for understanding the names of people one has encountered either in person or through the media. I understand that a sentence involving the name "Barack Obama" is true just if the person whose face I can recognize is as the sentence says he is.

2.5. Summary

The Expressibility Principle suggests that we can give an account of "I"-thoughts through thinking about what is involved in using and understanding "I"-sentences. This chapter has proposed a general framework for thinking about linguistic understanding based on Frege's notion of sense. This framework is intended to be compatible with the Russell/Mill model of names as directly referential, since the proposed model of sense is not intended to answer the question of how the semantic values of names are fixed.

The senses of linguistic expressions are what competent language-users understand when they understand those expressions. The level of the sentence is fundamental, because truth is fundamental to understanding and it is sentences that have truth conditions. Understanding sub-sentential expressions is a matter of understanding how they contribute to determining the truth-conditions of sentences in which they feature. To understand "*a* is *F*" is to know what would count as *a* being *F*, where this in turn requires thinking of *a* in a particular way (under a particular mode of presentation), as well as knowledge of what it is for an arbitrary object to be *F*.

Chapter 3 looks at how this approach to sense and understanding has been applied to the first person "I" by Frege himself and, more recently, by Gareth Evans.

3
Frege and Evans on the Sense of "I"

So far I have argued, first, that we need to elucidate "I"-thoughts through an account of what it is to understand the first person pronoun "I" and, second, that the Fregean notion of sense provides the best available account of linguistic understanding (even for proponents of the Russell/Mill approach to propositions). This chapter starts putting these two ideas together, looking at different proposals for how indexicals in general, and the first person pronoun in particular, can be accommodated within a broadly Fregean framework.

Section 3.1 briefly reviews Frege's own programmatic remarks on "I" before discussing the challenges that indexicals have been thought to pose for Fregeans. I focus in particular on John Perry's claim that the only Fregean way of accommodating indexicals is to fractionate Frege's unitary notion of sense into two distinct entities, each with a different explanatory role. I explain why Perry's argument is not convincing and then go on, in section 3.2, to outline the general approach to the theory of sense and the detailed account of the sense of "I" proposed by Gareth Evans. This account will be the starting point for discussion in future chapters.

3.1. Indexicals and Fregean Thoughts: Challenges and Opportunities

Indexical expressions are context-sensitive. The object picked out by an indexical is a function of the context in which the expression is uttered. In the case of demonstratives such as "this" or "that," the object referred to is most frequently determined by the ostensive gesture accompanying the utterance (or by whatever else makes a particular object peculiarly salient in that context). Simple rules determine a particular person as the referent of token-reflexive expressions such as "I" and "you"—roughly, "I" refers to the utterer of the sentence and "you" to the person (or persons) addressed.[1]

Given that indexical expressions have varying reference, any account of their sense confronts a stark choice. Does a given indexical have a single sense holding across different contexts of utterance, or does it have a different sense for each different context of utterance? For the first person pronoun, is there a single sense of "I" or is each person's use of "I" to refer to himself associated with a different sense of "I"? There are pressures in each direction. On the one hand, it seems plausible to demand that what I understand when I hear you saying "I am hungry" is the same as what you understand when you hear me say "I am hungry." There is a sense on which we are saying the same thing. But on the other, if sense determines reference and reference varies with context, then there cannot be a single sense of "I." But what then happens to the basic idea driving this book that we can explain the distinctive role and behavior of "I"-thoughts through an account of the sense of the first person pronoun "I"?

Frege's own discussion of "I" does nothing to resolve these difficulties. In fact it introduces new challenges. His only published

---

[1] Terminology is not always consistent in this area. Some authors use "indexical" as the generic category, while others (such as Kaplan) use "demonstrative." I will use "indexical" to include demonstratives, disambiguating where appropriate.

discussion of the first person pronoun is in his late paper "Thought," where he applies the model of sense as mode of presentation quite literally to "I":

> Everyone is presented to himself in a special and primitive way, in which he is presented to no one else. So, when Dr Lauben has the thought that he was wounded, he will probably be basing it on this primitive way in which he is presented to himself.[2]

But only Dr Lauben can grasp thoughts of this type. Frege continues, therefore:

> But now he may want to communicate with others. He cannot communicate a thought he alone can grasp. Therefore, if he now says "I was wounded", he must use "I" in a sense which can be grasped by others, perhaps in the sense of "he who is speaking to you at this moment"; by doing this he makes the conditions accompanying his utterance serve towards the expression of a thought.[3]

So, for Frege, there are two different thoughts, of fundamentally different types—a private thought graspable only by Dr Lauben, and a public thought communicable to others. Both thoughts are expressible using "I"—the first using what might be termed the "I" of soliloquy and the second the "I" of communication.[4] Taking the sense of "I" to be what is understood by someone who understands a sentence involving "I," Frege suggests that "I" has two distinct senses. The private sense of "I" is, quite literally, a mode of presentation of the self to itself. Only with respect to its private sense is "I" expressive of self-awareness.[5] The public sense of "I" has nothing to do with self-awareness. It is purely a matter of understanding the linguistic-behavior of the first person pronoun (its token-reflexivity).

---

[2] Frege 1918b, p. 333.   [3] Frege 1918b, p. 333.
[4] The terminology originates in Dummett 1981, p. 123.
[5] But see May 2006, particularly n. 34, for an argument that Frege did *not* propose a private sense for "I."

This is rather mysterious. Unsurprisingly, indexicals are widely viewed as the Achilles heel for Fregean sense. Kaplan's highly influential work has convinced many that indexicals are primary exhibits for the Russell/Mill model of referring expressions.[6] Kaplan provides an elegant formal treatment that treats both demonstratives (such as "that) and pure indexicals (such as "I," "now," and "here") as devices of direct reference. His work is generally viewed as one of the two pillars of the Russell/Mill model, the other of course being Kripke's attack on descriptivist models of proper names.

Even authors more generally sympathetic to Frege's notion of sense have thought that indexicals pose significant challenges. Richard Heck, who accepts a view of Fregean sense very similar to that laid out in the previous chapter, thinks that sentences containing indexicals cannot express Fregean thoughts, for reasons that are ultimately based on arguments from communication.[7] We will come back to Heck's views further when we discuss linguistic communication.

John Perry has argued that properly accommodating indexicals requires fractionating Frege's unitary notion of sense into two. In "Frege on demonstratives" he draws a distinction between the notion of sense, on the one hand, and the notion of a thought, on the other.[8] Since one of the principal drivers for our discussion of the sense of "I" is explaining the cognitive role of "I"-thoughts, as encapsulated in the two essential indexicality theses discussed in

---

[6] Kaplan 1989, a paper that had been circulating in various forms for nearly two decades before appearing in print in Almog, Perry, and Wettstein 1989, which also contains other important discussions of the semantics of indexicals. See also Schiffer 1981; Recanati 1993; Corazza 2004; and Recanati 2007. Swimming against the current, Salmon 2002 tries to apply what he terms Frege's Solution to Frege's Puzzle (as defended in his 1986) to demonstratives. Salmon's Fregeanism is rather different from that discussed here.

[7] Heck 2002. But see May 2006 for an attempt to rehabilitate a Fregean account of indexicals.

[8] Perry 1977. Perry uses somewhat different terminology in "The essential indexical" (Perry 1979), where "sense" is replaced by "belief state" and "thought" by "belief."

Frege and Evans on the Sense of "I" ~ 45

Chapter 1, it is particularly interesting that his primary motivation for fractionating the notion of sense is to account for the role of "I"-thoughts in explaining action.

We use senses to individuate psychological states, in explaining and predicting action. It is the sense entertained, not the thought apprehended, that is tied to human action. When you and I entertain the sense of "a bear is about to attack me", we behave similarly. We both roll up in a ball and try to be as still as possible. Different thoughts apprehended, same sense entertained, same behavior. When you and I both apprehend the thought that I am about to be attacked by a bear, we behave differently. I roll up in a ball, you run to get help. Same thought apprehended, different sense entertained, different behavior.[9]

The very person picked out by the first person pronoun is part of the content of a belief expressed by a sentence involving "I"—and the thoughts expressed by two different persons each uttering equiform tokens of a given "I"-sentence are correspondingly different. But two people will respond in the same way to the sentence "a bear is about to attack me," even though that sentence gives rise in each of them to a different belief. The notion of sense captures what leads these two people to behave in similar ways.

For Perry the sense of a sentence containing an indexical expression does not shift with the context. The sense of a simple sentence of the form "I am F" is composed of the incomplete sense of the predicate "F" conjoined with an element corresponding to the linguistic rule that a token of "I" refers to the utterer of that token. The *thought* expressed by the utterance of an indexical expression, on the other hand, is closer to a Russell/Mill proposition (a singular thought). It is composed of the actual object picked out by the relevant indexical expression, together with the sense of the relevant predicate expression (as opposed to the property denoted by that predicate expression, which would be a more standard way of developing the Russell/Mill approach).

---

[9] Perry 1977, pp. 494–5.

Perry's basic move counterintuitively sacrifices the basic tenet of propositional attitude psychology that people act the way they do because of what they believe. In his view, what people believe (the content of their belief) does not directly explain how they behave. My belief that I am about to be attacked by a bear is a belief about me (and correspondingly different from your belief that you are about to be attacked by a bear) and this fact can only be captured at the level of the thought expressed by the indexical sentence "I am about to be attacked by a bear." But the fact that the sentence "I am about to be attacked by a bear" is about me, as opposed to you, is not in Perry's view a part of the explanation of why a certain type of behavior is correlated with uttering that sentence.

The content of an indexical belief, according to Perry, is an object-dependent proposition. This object-dependent proposition is what is either true or false. The bearers of truth and falsity are also what feature in inferences. This is most obvious when the inferences are truth functional. If the validity of an inference is a function of the truth values of its constituents, then those constituents must be truth apt. But the constituents of truth-functional inferences must also be capable of featuring in non-truth-functional inferences.

Thinking about belief and inference makes clear that Perry's position is unacceptable. He holds that the things to which we appeal in giving psychological explanations of behavior are not the things over which inferences are defined. This makes it impossible to make sense of the idea of a person reasoning their way toward acting in a certain way. The conclusion of a practical inference must be an object-dependent proposition. This is so because your practical inference leads to a different conclusion from mine, and object-dependent propositions (what Perry calls thoughts) are intended to mark this difference. So, let us suppose that this practical inference issues in action. It is natural to think that an adequate explanation of the relevant action will correctly identify the conclusion of the practical inference. And yet this is precisely

Frege and Evans on the Sense of "I" ~ 47

what Perry is committed to denying, because he thinks that, in his terminology, senses not thoughts explain actions.[10]

So what has gone wrong? Perry's argument rests on two implicit principles. The first is that all tokens of a given behavior-type require the same explanation. The second is that giving the same explanation for two different behavior-tokens of the same type involves attributing the same psychological states to the authors of the two behaviors. These two principles rule out giving explanations of different tokens of a given behavior-type in terms of object-dependent propositions—provided, of course, that we really do have different tokens of a given behavior-type in the cases that Perry discusses.

Perry is assuming that if our bodies move in comparable ways then we are behaving in the same way, so that there is just one behavior that is instantiated both when you roll yourself up in a ball and when I roll myself up in a ball. It is true that there is a way of thinking about behavior on which this is indeed the case. This is the sense of "behavior" on which a behavior is just a series of bodily movements. But psychological explanations explain *actions* rather than bodily movements, and actions are (at least partially) individuated by their goal. From this perspective it is not obvious

---

[10] It is important to clear up a potential confusion. Perry draws a close parallel between his notion of sense and Kaplan's notion of character (Kaplan 1989). Kaplan, like Perry, fractionates the notion of thought into two components—character and content (to be discussed in more detail in the next chapter). Kaplan has developed a logic of demonstratives in which the notion of character plays an integral part. However, Kaplan's logic of demonstratives is perfectly compatible with my claims about the split between inferences and psychological explanation. Although Kaplan's character (Perry's sense) does feature in his logic of demonstratives, it does so in a very subordinate role. Kaplan holds that the character of a linguistic expression is given by linguistic rules such as those deployed in the recursive definitions that serve to define truth and denotation in a context. There are no inferences at the level of character, although we need character to identify the objects over which inferences are defined and evaluated. Truth and validity only arise with reference to specific contexts, whereas the whole point of the notion of character is that it abstracts away from the specifics of context. (I am grateful to Chris Gauker for encouraging me to address this issue.)

that my rolling up in a ball is the same action as your rolling up in a ball. After all, my rolling myself up in a ball is intended to save *me* from the bear, while your rolling yourself up in a ball is intended to save *you* from the bear. In this case we have two different actions effected by similar sets of bodily movements.[11] If one looks at the matter like this then Perry's two principles do not yield the same result. What I am doing is saving myself from the bear. This action-type can have other tokens, such as, for example, my shooting the bear. These tokens would, in accordance with Perry's two principles, have the same explanation, namely, my belief that I am about to be attacked by a bear. Your rolling yourself up into a ball is a token of a completely different action-type, namely the action-type of your saving yourself from the bear, and like the other tokens of that type it is to be explained in terms of your belief that you are about to be attacked by a bear.

Certainly, our actions are related. But this does not mean that there is a single thing (in Perry's vocabulary—the sense of the sentence "I am about to be attacked by a bear") that explains both our behaviors. Consider the proposition expressed by the sentence "JLB is about to be attacked by a bear" (leaving open for the moment whether that proposition is to be understood in Perry's way or in some other way). We see that proposition as made up of an element corresponding to the proper name "JLB" and a propositional function corresponding to the incomplete expression "— is about to be attacked by a bear." Both my thought that I am about to be attacked by a bear and your thought that you are about to be attacked by a bear involve that very same propositional function being completed by constituents that in some sense correspond to the first person pronoun we might use to express our beliefs. Surely the fact that both thoughts can be interpreted in terms of a single propositional function captures the respect in which they are similar.

---

[11] Compare Evans (1982, pp. 203–4).

To take stock: The overarching project, underwritten by the Expressibility Principle, of elucidating "I"-thoughts through giving an account of the sense of "I" requires, *pace* Perry, that (in the case of indexicals in general and "I" in particular) there must be a single thing that does the explanatory work that Perry parcels out between thought and sense. Frege's own account of "I" provides little guidance. In the next section, therefore, we will turn to the best developed account of the (unitary) sense of "I," that developed by Gareth Evans.

3.2. Evans on the Sense of "I"

In order to understand fully what Evans says about "I" we need to start with his overarching account of sense, developed primarily in his posthumously published book *The Varieties of Reference*.[12]

As noted in Chapter 2, the Fregean sense of a referring expression is standardly taken to be a definite description or cluster of definite descriptions. The referring expression refers to a given object because that object is the unique satisfier of the associated description or cluster of descriptions. This way of understanding how sense determines reference has been subjected to a battery of criticisms, many of which have to do with what are taken to be its counterintuitive modal implications. According to Kripke, the prime instigator, referring expressions such as proper names are rigid designators, which is to say that they refer to the same object in all possible worlds (in which that object exists) whereas definite descriptions are nonrigid designators that can shift reference across possible worlds.

The repudiation of the descriptive view is central to Evans's development of the notion of sense, which also treats proper

---

[12] Evans 1982. For an overview of Evans's overall philosophical contributions see the introduction and essays in Bermúdez 2005c.

names and nondescriptive referring expressions as rigid designators.[13] Evans takes his lead from what he calls Russell's Principle, according to which a subject cannot make a judgment about something unless he knows which object his judgment is about. Evans interprets "knowing which" as requiring that the thinker possess *discriminating knowledge* of the object being thought about.[14] We have, he maintains, an intuitive grasp of three different forms that such discriminating knowledge might take. A thinker might possess discriminating knowledge of an object by perceiving it. Or by being able to recognize it.[15] Or by knowing distinguishing facts about it. Each way of possessing discriminating knowledge corresponds to a distinct type of linguistic referring expression.

The discriminating knowledge that derives from standing in a perceptual relation to an object will most obviously be linguistically expressed by means of demonstrative expressions (understanding demonstratives narrowly, as expressions whose reference is fixed through pointing or another way of directing the audience's attention). The understanding of most proper names will deploy recognitional discriminating knowledge, while knowledge of discriminating facts about an object will most naturally be linguistically expressed through definite descriptions. For Evans different types of referring expression are correlated with different ways of identifying objects: demonstratives with perceptual identification; (most) proper names with recognitional identification; and definite descriptions (and some proper names) with identification through satisfaction.

Most of *The Varieties of Reference* is devoted to recognitional and perceptual identification, both of which rest upon the thinker's

---

[13] Evans allows a category of so-called descriptive names that function as rigid designators although their reference is fixed descriptively. See Evans 1982, §2.3.

[14] Evans 1982, p. 89.

[15] It is not simply perceptual recognition that is at stake here. Evans is operating with a broad sense of recognition that extends, for example, to recognizing information that would be relevant to determining the truth value of sentences about the object. This is now he would deal with names of historical persons for example.

standing in certain information-links to the object being thought about. These information-links yield the thinker's discriminating knowledge (or what Evans calls the subject's Idea, a conception of the object that allows the thinker to differentiate that object from all other objects). In the case of demonstrative referring expressions these information links are perceptual, but Evans envisages a far wider range of information links in the case of recognition-based thoughts, including information-links based upon memory and testimony. In each case the sense of the relevant expression is understood (partially) in terms of the ability to exploit the relevant information links.[16]

Evans discusses "I" in two different places. In "Understanding demonstratives" Evans offers an account of the sense of "I" in the context of a general discussion of demonstratives.[17] In *The Varieties of Reference* Evans devotes an entire chapter to self-identification. There he investigates what he calls each person's "I"-idea—the discriminating knowledge of oneself that allows one to think "I"-thoughts. An "I"-thought, according to Evans, is a thought typically expressed through a sentence containing the first person pronoun, and so what Evans says about "I"-ideas can be taken to represent his views about the sense of the first person pronoun, entirely in line with the view so far developed in this book.

One way of interpreting Evans on "I" is as interpreting Frege's famous phrase that "everyone is presented to himself in a special and primitive way in which he is presented to no one else" in terms of the general thesis that the sense of a referring expression is to be understood in terms of the utterer's discriminating knowledge of the referent of that expression. Everyone who uses the first person pronoun with understanding does so in virtue of ways they have of

---

[16] A somewhat similar picture has been developed by John Campbell, particularly for the sense of perceptual demonstratives. See Campbell 2002.
[17] Evans 1981.

thinking about themselves that are both primitive and not available to anyone else.

Using the first person pronoun to refer to oneself requires being in touch with a particular object (namely, oneself), but not in a way that involves picking oneself out as the referent of the pronoun. Rather, it involves being in receipt of certain types of information—information that is distinctive in virtue precisely of being the sort of information that does *not* require identification of a particular object as the source of that information. The types of information that canonically underpin self-reference on Evans's theory have the property, originally discussed by Sydney Shoemaker, of giving rise to judgments that are *immune to error through misidentification relative to the first person pronoun* (henceforth; the IEM property).[18]

A judgment "I am F" with the IEM property in virtue of the information on which it is based is not susceptible to a particular type of error. The person making the judgment cannot be mistaken about whom or what it is that is being judged to be F. Alternatively put, there is no gap between learning that someone is F and learning that one is oneself F. There is no such gap because these judgments are made in ways that do not involve identifying a particular person as oneself. They are, in Evans's phrase, identification-free.

So, for example, introspection might lead me to believe that I am having a certain thought. I may well be mistaken, but I cannot be mistaken about who it is whom I am taking to be having that thought. Likewise, my field of view is structured in a way that offers information about my spatial relations to perceived objects and about the route I am taking through the perceived

---

[18] Shoemaker 1968. For different formulations and interpretations of the IEM property see, for example, Wright 1998; Pryor 1999; Coliva 2006; and the essays in Prosser and Recanati 2012.

environment.[19] This information might be inaccurate but it cannot (in the normal course of events) be information about anyone else's (apparent) spatial location or trajectory.

Many first person judgments lack the IEM property. Evans analyzes these identification-dependent judgments in terms of a pair of judgments "I am μ" and "μ is F," where "μ" is some way of picking out or identifying a person. On pain of regress, the judgment "I am μ" must either itself be IEM or analyzable at some point into a pair of judgments, one of which has the IEM property.[20]

Let "I" be an identification-free way of thinking of the self and "I*" denote an identification-dependent way of thinking of the self (e.g. "the person currently being addressed" or "the shopper who is spilling sugar"). An identification-dependent judgment will typically take the form "I* is F." As emphasized in the theses of essential indexicality maintained by Perry and others and discussed in Chapter 1, this judgment will only motivate me to act (so that I answer the question, or look for the hole in the bag of sugar) when I realize that I am the person being thought about. In short, I need to realize that I am I*. This is an identity judgment where what is being grasped is that a single object (me) is being thought about in two different ways—an identification-free way and an identification-dependent way. The identification-dependent way of thinking of myself is brought into the ambit of self-conscious thought by the identification-free way of thinking about myself. These identity judgments themselves have the IEM property. The judgment "I am I*" may be mistaken, but not because it turns out to be someone other than myself whom I take to be I*. (Of course, if the identify judgment is false then its second term should more properly be described as an identification-dependent way of thinking of someone mistakenly identified as the self.)

---

[19] Bermúdez 1998, 2003b.   [20] Evans 1982, pp. 80–1.

Judgments with the IEM property are made on the basis of certain, very specific information-sources, including:

- *introspection* (information about occurrent thoughts and mental states);
- *somatic proprioception and kinesthesis* (information derived from bodily awareness about limb position and bodily movement);
- *visual kinesthesis* (visually derived information about movement and spatial relations to perceived objects);
- *autobiographical memory* (information about one's past derived from remembered episodes in one's personal history).

All of these information-sources can give rise to first person judgments that are identification-free, because they present information in such a way that it could not but be about the self. If somatic proprioception tells me that legs are crossed, it can only be my legs that are crossed. If through introspection I encounter a thought about Bavaria, it can only be me who is thinking about Bavaria.

There is an identifiable class of first person judgments corresponding to each information source. First person judgments grounded in introspection and somatic proprioception typically report psychological states and bodily dispositions respectively. Similarly for visual kinesthesis, which tends to underpin judgments of spatial position and movement. Autobiographical memories generally give rise either to memory reports ("I remember going swimming") or to first person past-tense judgments ("I went swimming").

There has been much discussion of whether all of these different classes of judgment really do have the IEM property. Shoemaker, for example, raises the possibility of quasi-memories that are phenomenologically indistinguishable from genuine memories, but that have a different causal ancestry and in fact originate in someone else's personal history.[21] The possibility of quasi-memories shows,

---

[21] Shoemaker 1970. Compare Parfit 1984 at pp. 220–2. For discussion see McDowell 1997 and Burge 2003a.

according to Shoemaker, that memory judgments do not have the IEM property. However, Shoemaker's reasoning is ultimately unconvincing.[22] I will adopt the (plausible) assumptions, first, that quasi-memories are not live possibilities in our current world and, second, that nobody has good reasons for thinking that their memories might be quasi-memories. Given those two assumptions, memory judgments have the IEM property because the memories on which they are based are presented to us as our own memories and can be taken at face value, since there is no reason to think that they are not our own memories.[23] The same holds for first person judgments made on the basis of proprioception. It seems possible for two individuals to have their bodies "cross-wired," so that proprioceptively derived information from one would be picked up by the other.[24] If such a situation were sufficiently widespread then proprioceptively based first person judgments would be identification-dependent. But since it is not, such judgments have the IEM property, at least in a de facto and circumstantial sense (to use Shoemaker's own terminology).

We can see how Evans proposes to develop Frege's suggestion that "everyone is presented to himself in a special and primitive way in which he is presented to no one else." Understanding Frege's "way of being presented to oneself" as involving ways of thinking of oneself (in line with his general way of understanding what Frege says about modes of presentation), Evans elucidates what is "special and primitive" in terms of the capacity to think thoughts, and to make statements, that are immune to error

[22] See Bermúdez forthcoming-b.
[23] This applies only to explicit memory judgments—e.g. judgments of the form "I remember φ-ing." As we will see in more detail in Chapter 8 below, past-tense judgments of the form "I φ-ed" are much more complicated, and need not have IEM status, even when grounded in autobiographical memory. For further discussion of memory and the IEM property see Hamilton 1995, 2007.
[24] As originally proposed in Armstrong 1984, p. 113. For further discussion of the IEM property and judgments based on somatic proprioception see Cassam 1995; Bermúdez 2005a, 2011b; Newstead 2006; Schwenkler 2013; and de Vignemont 2011.

through misidentification relative to the first person pronoun. The sense of the first person pronoun is the ability to keep in touch with the person that one in fact is, the person referred to by one's use of the first person pronoun. This ability is a function of one's possessing sources of information about oneself that are immune to error through misidentification.

There are two further dimensions to Evans's account of the first person. One has to do with the "output" side of first person judgments. Being appropriately in touch with the person one in fact is is a function of one's ability to act on judgments derived from the appropriate information sources. Evans's account speaks directly to the issues about psychological explanation and cognitive dynamics raised by Perry. When I acquire information that is suitably immune to error through misidentification to the effect that there is a bear coming toward me then I act in the appropriate manner, immediately and without needing to identify myself as the person toward whom the bear is coming. There is no room for the thought that might be expressed "the bear is coming toward someone, but is that me?" and no delay in moving straight into action. It might turn out that the bear has designs on the person behind me, rather than on me, but this would not be an error of misidentification in the required sense. It would be a mistake about the ramifications of the fact that the bear is coming toward me.

The final strand in his account of "I"-ideas departs both from Frege and from considerations of functional role, as standardly understood.

Indispensable though these familiar ingredients (an information component and an action component) are in any account of the Ideas we have of ourselves, ... they cannot constitute an exhaustive account of our "I"-ideas. So long as we focus on judgements which a person might make about himself on the basis of the relevant ways of gaining knowledge, the inadequacy may not strike us. A subject's knowledge of what it is for the thought "I am in pain" to be true may appear to be exhausted by his capacity to decide, simply upon the basis of how he feels, whether or not it is true—and similarly in the case of all the other ways of gaining knowledge about ourselves. However, our view of ourselves is not Idealistic: we are perfectly capable of grasping propositions about ourselves which we are quite incapable of deciding, or even offering grounds for. I can grasp the thought that I was breast-fed, for example, or that I was unhappy on my first birthday, or that I tossed and turned in my sleep last night, or that I shall be dragged unconscious through the streets of Chicago, or that I shall die.[25]

We can, Evans emphasizes, effectively think about ourselves from a third-person point of view, entertaining possibilities to which we have no informational links (as in the vivid examples he gives). The truth conditions of these thoughts are far more complex than the truth conditions of thoughts about oneself that are based upon introspection, proprioception and other information-sources that are immune to error through misidentification.

Consider a sentence of the form "I am F," where "F" is a predicate whose applicability to oneself can be determined through one of the informational links we have been discussing—and hence where the sentence as a whole has the IEM property. The truth condition for "I am F" is intimately tied to the subject's ability to use the relevant information link to determine whether the predicate applies. Because "I am F" is immune to error through misidentification, the subject does not have to identify himself in order to grasp the truth condition of the thought that the sentence expresses—the thought will be true just if the subject can detect F-relevant information in the favored way. The issue, from the subject's point of view, is simply whether or not there is F-ness. But when it comes to "I am F" sentences that do not have the IEM property the subject's grasp of the truth condition must involve, not simply sensitivity to the presence or absence of

---

[25] Evans 1982, pp. 208–9.

F-ness, but an ability to determine what it would be for it to be he who is F. And this in turn means that the subject must be able to think of himself in a much richer way than is required in order to grasp the truth condition of sentences that are immune to error through misidentification.

Evans returns at this point to Russell's principle and to the idea that thinking about an object involves having discriminating knowledge of that object. For Evans this requirement holds no less when the object in question is oneself than when it is an object in the distal environment. So, the final strand in Evans's account of "I"-ideas (and hence of the sense of the first person pronoun) is that the thinker possess discriminating knowledge of himself, where this knowledge is understood in terms of the subject's ability to locate himself within the objective spatio-temporal world.[26] Here is how Evans puts it.

> It seems to me clear that as we conceive of persons, they are distinguished from one another by fundamental grounds of difference of the same kind as those which distinguish other physical things, and that a fundamental identification of a person involves a consideration of him as the person occupying such-and-such a spatio-temporal location. Consequently, to know what it is for [δ = I] to be true, for arbitrary δ, is to know what is involved in locating oneself in a spatio-temporal map of the world.[27]

Being able to locate herself within a spatio-temporal map of the world allows a thinker to determine the truth condition of any thought (whether that thought involves predicates that are susceptible to error through misidentification, or immune to such error). With this third dimension in his account of "I"-ideas Evans moves away from Frege and closer to a broadly Kantian conception of self-conscious thought, in which the ability to think about oneself is

---

[26] See Evans 1982, section 7.1 and the appendix to Chapter 7.
[27] Evans 1982, p. 211.

Frege and Evans on the Sense of "I" ~ 59

intimately tied to the ability to think about the objective order of things.[28]

3.3. Summary

Frege's thoughts on the sense of the first person pronoun are more suggestive than illuminating and a number of authors have argued that indexicals cannot be accommodated within a Fregean theory of sense. Perry, for example, argues that the role of indexicals in motivating and explaining action forces apart two strands in Frege's notion of sense. In his view there is no single category of "I"-thoughts that can serve both as the senses of assertoric sentences involving "I" and as the objects of belief, desire, and other propositional attitudes. After finding Perry's argument wanting we reviewed the most developed account of the (unitary) sense of "I" currently available—that of Gareth Evans. Evans's account, based on his distinctive interpretation of Frege's notion of sense, analyzes the sense of "I" in terms of three components

- an input component (understood through the capacity to think thoughts that have the IEM property because they are based on introspection, autobiographical memory, somatic proprioception, or visual kinesthesis);
- an output property (understood through "I"-thoughts being immediately relevant to action, as suggested by the theses of essential indexicality);
- an objectivity component (understood through the subject's ability to take a third-person perspective on her own spatiotemporal location in the world).

The next chapter will examine Evans's account of the sense of "I" more critically.

---

[28] This aspect of Evans's view has been taken in Campbell 1994; Cassam 1997; and Bermúdez 1998. The original inspiration is of course Strawson 1959 (and ultimately Kant's *Critique of Pure Reason*).

4
Privacy, Objectivity, Symmetry

For Frege the sense of "I" is private and unshareable. When Dr Lauben, or anyone else for that matter, bases a thought on the "special and primitive way in which he is presented to himself," Frege describes that thought as "one that he alone can grasp," and hence one that cannot be communicated. This is at odds with other strands in his thinking about thought and language—both on his frequently emphasized separation between thoughts as objective entities independent of individual thinkers and their psychological vagaries, and on the idea that linguistic understanding can be elucidated through the theory of sense.

Evans's account of the sense of "I" follows Frege in this respect, explicitly affirming that the sense of "I" is private. Sources of self-specifying information, such as introspection and proprioception, give rise to judgments with the IEM property precisely because they are accessible only to the thinker. This is also why they have direct and immediate implications for action. Evans tries to argue that a private sense of "I" as private can nonetheless be objective. I evaluate this argument in section 4.1 and find it unsatisfactory. Section 4.2 offers positive arguments against any account of the sense of "I" that holds it to be private and unshareable, defending what I term the Symmetry Constraint, according to which any account of the sense of "I" must allow for tokens of "I" and "you" to have the same sense in appropriate contexts. I offer three arguments for the Symmetry Constraint—an argument from same-saying and reported speech; an argument from the nature of denial and disagreement; and an argument from the epistemology of testimony.

4.1. Privacy and Objectivity

Evans explicitly endorses Frege's suggestion that the sense of "I" is private. Whereas Perry, for example, states that "nothing could be more out of the spirit of Frege's account of sense and thought that an incommunicable, private thought,"[1] Evans claims that Frege's privacy thesis is perfectly compatible with his overarching conception of thought, arguing that the privacy of "I"-thoughts is independently motivated.

For Evans Frege's fundamental desideratum is objectivity, which he thinks is perfectly compatible with "I"-thoughts being private.

> What is absolutely fundamental to Frege's philosophy of language is that thoughts should be *objective*—that the existence of a thought should be independent of its being thought by anyone, and hence that thoughts are to be distinguished from *ideas* or the contents of a particular consciousness. When Frege stresses that thoughts can be grasped by several people, it is usually to emphasize that it is not like an idea.
>
> A true thought was true before it was grasped by anyone. A thought does not have to be owned by anyone. The same thought can be grasped by several people.
>
> His most extended treatment of the nature of thoughts—"The Thought"—makes it clear that it is the inference from shareability to objectivity which is of paramount importance to Frege, rather than shareability itself. Since an unshareable thought can be perfectly objective—can exist and

---

[1] Perry 1977, p. 474.

have a truth value independently of anyone's entertaining it—there is no clash between what Frege says about "I"-thoughts and this, undeniably central, aspect of his philosophy.[2]

In the first part of the passage Evans talks about private thoughts being objective in virtue of not being reducible to the contents of an individual consciousness—and in the second part he suggests that objective, private thoughts can exist and have a truth value independently of anyone entertaining them. There is really only one core idea here, though. The most obvious way to make sense of the idea of a thought not being reducible to the contents of an individual consciousness is through the thought being shareable (i.e. thinkable by others). With that option unavailable the only way for a thought to be irreducible would be to exist and have a truth value independently of anyone entertaining it.

There certainly are thoughts that fit this description—e.g. mathematical thoughts, provided that you are not a constructivist about mathematics. But could private "I"-thoughts be amongst them? It would seem not, given that the identity of any given "I"-thought is a function of the episode of thinking. The whole point of token-reflexivity, and indexicality in general, is that the identity of the thought is determined by the context in which it is thought—in which case, there is no thought without an episode of thinking. If this episode has to be an episode featuring the subject of the thought (as it must be if the thought is nonshareable), then the thought cannot exist and have a truth value independently of being thought by the particular person who is the subject of the thought.

Daniel Morgan objects to an earlier version of this argument against Evans in the following interesting passage.

From the fact that context determines which indexical thought a mental utterance of an indexical sentence expresses, it does not follow that the

---

[2] Evans 1981, p. 313, quoting from Frege's posthumous essay, "My logical insights," Frege 1915, p. 251.

Privacy, Objectivity, Symmetry ~ 63

existence of an indexical thought depends on someone or other's actually having produced a mental utterance which expresses that thought. Compare: which target, if any, at the fairground shooting stand one hits depends on which direction one aims in. But it would be a non sequitur to conclude that the existence of a particular target depends on someone or other's actually having fired a shot which hits that target. If there is a slack day at the fair and no one fires a shot which is aimed in the right direction to hit a particular target, that target can still exist. The whole point of indexicality may be that the identity of an indexical thought expressed by a particular indexical vehicle is determined by the context in which that indexical vehicle is produced. But this does not show that there can be no indexical thought without an indexical vehicle, i.e., without an episode of thinking.[3]

Morgan denies that an "I"-thought is constituted by a particular episode of thinking in a particular context. The context-sensitive episode of thinking simply determines which of a range of possible (and independently existing) "I"-thoughts gives the content of the episode of thinking. The episode of thinking stands to the content of thought as the shot does to the target, rather than as (to extend his analogy) the pulling of the trigger does to the firing of the shot. And, just as the target can exist without any shot being fired, so too can "I"-thoughts exist (and presumably have truth values) without any episodes of indexical thinking.

It is clear that Morgan (and Evans) want to say that, even though I did not at noon today think that I myself was tired, there is an "I"-thought that would have been the content of my episode of thinking, had there been one, and that thought has a truth value (false, as it happens). That "I"-thought includes a private sense corresponding to the distinctive way in which I am presented to myself. Its identity depends (of course) on my existence and my being presented to myself in the way that I am. But neither its identity nor its truth value depends upon the episode of thinking.

[3] Morgan 2009, responding to Bermúdez 2005b.

The problem with this proposal emerges when one asks how an episode of indexical thinking (or the utterance of an indexical sentence) fixes the truth condition of the associated thought. The defining characteristic of indexical thinking is that the episode of thinking fixes the truth condition of the thought through fixing the contextual parameters. It is the fact that a thinks "I am F here, now" at time t in location l that fixes the truth condition of the thought as a being F at time t in location l. It is certainly acceptable from a Fregean perspective to hold that there exists, independent of my or anyone else thinking it, a thought that is true if and only if a is F at time t in location l. But, *ex hypothesi*, those parameters are not fixed in the way that they would be were that the truth condition of an indexical thought. And for that reason they come out as different thoughts from a Fregean perspective. To see this apply Frege's intuitive criterion for the distinctness of thoughts, on which two utterances express different thoughts just if it is possible to take incompatible attitudes toward them. It is perfectly possible, for example, that a might be disposed to assent to "I am F (here, now)" at time t in location l, while thinking it false that "a is F at t in location l." All that would be required is that a be unaware of one or more of the following identities: I = a; t = now; or l = here.

Both Evans and Morgan are equivocating between the harmless (and true) proposition that

(1) There is an episode of thinking in context $<a, t, l>$ $\Box\!\!\rightarrow$ $\exists x$ [x is the content of that thought].

and the more substantial (and false) proposition that

(2) $\exists x$ [There is an episode of thinking in context $<a, t, l>$ $\Box\!\!\rightarrow$ x is the content of that thought].

In both (1) and (2) the "$\Box\!\!\rightarrow$" indicates a subjunctive conditional. This is appropriate because what we are talking about is whether there are indexical thoughts that exist independently of any episode of thinking—and so the antecedent in the conditionals in (1) and (2) will typically be false in the situations we are interested in. If (1) and (2) were formulated with material conditionals then they would be equivalent. But they are certainly not equivalent with subjunctive conditionals.[4]

So, we are assuming that there is no episode of thinking in context $<a, t, l>$. We should certainly accept that, were it to be true that there is an episode of context-sensitive thinking in context $<a, t, l>$, then there would be something that is the content of that context-sensitive episode of thinking. But it would be fallacious to conclude that there is something that would be the content of an episode of context-sensitive thinking in context $<a, t, l>$, were such an episode of thinking to take place. And in fact it is false that there would be, because without an episode of thinking there would be no way of setting the contextual parameters appropriately. What is acceptable is:

(3) $\exists x$ [There is an episode of thinking in context $<a, t, l>$ $\square\!\!\rightarrow$ x is the *truth condition* of that thought].

But that certainly does not give the result that Evans and Morgan seek, because it is at the level of reference rather than the level of sense.

4.2. *Privacy and Symmetry*

There are no prospects, then, for holding that private "I"-thoughts can be objective, in the sense of existing and having truth values independently of episodes of indexical thinking. But that still leaves open the question of whether the sense of "I" actually is private.

---

[4] As Quine puts it (1982, p. 143), crediting the phrase to Herbrand, there is a "rule of passage" allowing movement in both directions between the material conditionals $\exists x \,[p \rightarrow F(x)]$ and $p \rightarrow \exists x\, F(x)$. But there is no such rule of passage for subjunctive conditionals. To see this, take "$F(-)$" to denote "—is a flying horse" and let "p" be "$\exists y\, F(y)$."

To frame the issue, consider another well-known passage from Frege's essay "Thought" where he explicitly allows a degree of interchangeability between a thought expressed yesterday using "today" and a thought expressed today using "yesterday."

> If a time-indication is conveyed by the present tense one must know when the sentence is uttered in order to grasp the thought correctly. Therefore the time of utterance is part of the expression of the thought. If someone wants to say today what he expressed yesterday using the word "today" he will replace this word with "yesterday". Although the thought is the same its verbal expression must be different in order that the change of sense which would be otherwise be effected by differing times of utterance may be cancelled out.[5]

Evans coined the phrase "dynamic Fregean thoughts" for thoughts that permit comparable interchangeability.[6] Our question, therefore, is whether "I"-thoughts are dynamic Fregean thoughts. I shall argue that they are. "I"-thoughts can be expressed by sentences that do not contain the word "I" and that can be uttered by someone other than the subject of the "I"-thought. This has the immediate consequence that the sense of "I" cannot be a private sense.

A Fregean theory of sense is a theory of understanding. In a paper to which the argument that follows is deeply indebted Mark Sainsbury has emphasized the basic principle that in understanding a sentence I acquire knowledge of what that sentence says.[7] Of course, this is just one of the things that I can come to know through understanding a sentence. I can also come to know what the speaker intends to communicate, or what result it is likely to have (an inflammatory effect on the assembled crowd, for example). In each of these cases the knowledge that I acquire is typically knowledge that I can express. In the central case, where

---

[5] Frege 1918b, p. 332.
[6] On the more general problem of cognitive dynamics see the essays in Dokic 1997, Branquinho 1999, and Prosser 2005.
[7] Sainsbury 1998.

what I express is my knowledge of what is said, then I am, quite simply, reporting what is said. In the other, more complicated cases, what I am expressing goes beyond a report of what is said. It might be a report of communicative intent, or of perlocutionary effect.

As Sainsbury notes, if we confine ourselves to a language that does not contain indexicals, then when I report what is said I can typically do so using exactly the same words used in the original utterance (taking "utterance" in a broad sense that includes written inscriptions, and so on). Suppose, for example, that you say: "Harold is being characteristically damning." I can give a homophonic report of what you said, using exactly the same words after the "that—" clause as in the utterance being reported (modulo cosmetic changes in tense, and so on). This is plainly not possible when what is reported is perlocutionary effect. I might report the perlocutionary effect of your utterance as being that you reject Harold's assessment of the situation. Homophonic reports of perlucutionary effect are rarely appropriate. Reports of communicative intent fall somewhere in the middle. They can be homophonic, but the interesting cases tend to be the nonhomophonic ones. The cases where we can give a homophonic report of communicative intent are those where what the speaker intends to communicate is precisely what their utterance says, and here the notion of communicative intent as an independent factor drops out of the picture.

As soon as indexicality enters the picture, homophonic reports of what is said can no longer be expected in every case. Nonetheless, the bedrock status of homophonic reports in the nonindexical case points to an interesting and important feature of the central cases of reported speech, one that does extend to the indexical case. When a report is accurate, what is said by the words in which the report is couched can be mapped straightforwardly onto what is said by the words in the utterance being reported. The accuracy of a report is a function of the extent to which what it says (or rather: what is said by the elements of the report that report what is said, rather than who said it and when) is what was said by the utterance being reported. So, if we report a sentence through another sentence that says the same thing, then we can define equivalence classes of sentences under the same-saying relation—classes of sentences that say the same thing and hence can be used to accurately report each other. By the same token, the fact that one sentence accurately reports another is an indication that the two sentences fall into the same equivalence class.

Suppose, then, that you say to me: "Your position is either trivial or false." On being asked by a third party what you said to me I reply: "She said that my position is either trivial or false." This report is accurate. If the third party is aware of the background to the exchange, knows whom the personal pronouns pick out, and so on, then the knowledge that she gains through hearing my report of your utterance is precisely the knowledge that she would have acquired had she heard your original utterance. Were I to utter as a self-standing sentence the words following the "that—," namely "My position is either trivial or false," then I would make myself a samesayer with you, at least relative to that particular context of utterance. This is highly intuitive, given the logical relation between your saying "Your position is either trivial or false" and my saying "My position is neither trivial nor false." Plainly, what I am doing is denying what you are saying—in which case removing the negation sign makes us same-sayers.

This has interesting consequences for how we think about what is said by the indexicals in the respective utterances. If we are same-sayers then my token-utterance of "I" must stand in the same-saying relation to your token-utterance of "you." So, what we both understand when I say "I" (in that particular conversational context) must be the same as what we both understand when you say "you" in that context. And, since we are taking the notion of sense to be correlative to the notion of understanding, this means that the sense of "I" in that context must be the same as the sense of "you" in that context.

Privacy, Objectivity, Symmetry ~ 69

The point generalizes to give a basic constraint upon any satisfactory account of the sense of "I." What I term the *Symmetry Constraint* requires that we preserve the token-equivalence of "I" and other personal pronouns with respect to same-saying and relative to a particular context.

The Symmetry Constraint
An account of the sense of "I" must allow tokens of "I" to have the same sense as tokens of other personal pronouns such as "you" in appropriate contexts.

The Symmetry Constraint requires, for example, that any satisfactory account of the sense of "I" must make it possible for me to use "you" to report what you say using "I" (where the report and the original utterance are appropriately related). It is easiest to appreciate the symmetry constraint in the case of "I" and "you," but the constraint extends to other personal pronouns, most obviously "he" in the singular case, and "we," "you," and "they" in the plural case. Each of these personal pronouns can, *in suitable contexts*, be token-equivalent to another personal pronoun of the same number.

The qualification of context-dependence is important. It is not in general true that an accurate report of a speaker's indexical utterance can generate a single sentence that says the same thing as that indexical utterance. Sainsbury elegantly describes the characteristic feature of the nonindexical case as follows: "Within the simple picture of a single language and no indexicality, one who gave an adequate report could make himself a samesayer with the original speaker merely by uttering the words which follow 'said that' in his report."[8] As he himself illustrates, nothing like this holds generally once indexicals are brought into the picture. Accurately reporting indexical sentences involves setting the scene in ways that often

---

[8] Sainsbury 1998, p. 139.

prevent detaching the sentence that comes after the "that—" to give an utterance that says the same as the utterance being reported.

To give a simplified version of an example that Sainsbury discusses at some length, we might report Gareth Evans's utterance on July 4, 1968 of "today is July 4" by saying something along the lines of: "On July 4, 1968, Gareth Evans said that it was July 4." This report captures the indexicality of the original utterance, but there is no prospect of detaching the sentence following the "that—" to give an utterance that says the same as the original utterance. We cannot detach the sentence that gives the content of the sentence being reported because it is anaphorically dependent upon the preliminary scene-setting material. For an example involving "I" consider how we might report Dr Lauben's utterance on January 1, 1900 of the sentence "I am hungry." An accurate report would be "On January 1, 1900, intentionally speaking of himself, Dr Lauben said that he was hungry." Again, anaphoric dependence precludes detachability.

The token-equivalence that the Symmetry Constraint is intended to preserve applies primarily when fully explicit scene-setting is not required, because the reporter and the person to whom the report is addressed already possess the relevant information. Suppose that X says to me, on 10/1/2015: "My position is neither trivial nor false." I might report this at a later date to someone who was not present by saying something along these lines: "On 10/1/2015 X told me that her position was neither trivial nor false." We have the expected anaphoric dependence and failure of detachability. If you and I both know that we are talking about a conversation between X and me on 10/1/2015, however, then there is no need for scene-setting. I might simply say, "She said that her position is neither trivial nor false." The second indexical pronoun is not anaphorically dependent upon the first. Rather, the very same contextual facts and shared information that fix the reference of the first pronoun fix the reference of the second. So, I can detach the sentence "her position is neither trivial nor false" in a way that makes me a same-sayer with X's original utterance. This is exactly the sort of case to which the Symmetry Constraint applies. The account we give of how an understanding of X's use of "my" contributes to what is understood by X's utterance of "My position is neither trivial nor false" needs to allow me to be a same-sayer by uttering "His position is neither trivial nor false" in the relevant context.

The motivation for the Symmetry Constraint so far has come from considerations of same-saying and reported speech. There are two other important motivations, however. One is logical and the other is epistemological.

The logical motivation is straightforward. The possibility of equivalence in sense between first and second person pronouns is required for meaningful disagreement. If you say "What you claim is false" and I say "What I claim is not false" then I seem to be denying what you are asserting. Certainly it is not possible for our two utterances both to be true. That alone is not enough to warrant any conclusions about sameness of sense. It would not work for "Hesperus is Venus and "Phosphorus is not Venus," for example. But here, unlike the Hesperus/Phosphorus case, we can apply a Fregean criterion for sameness of thought. No bystander listening to our conversation and able to identify the referents of the first and second person pronouns could possibly assign both utterances the same truth value, which suggests that there is one thing (the claim that I am making) that I hold to be true and you hold to be false. What I am saying is the negation of what you have just said. But then, in this context, my utterance of "I" and your utterance of "you" must have the same sense.

This argument might be resisted on the grounds that logical relations hold at the level of reference not at the level of sense. In Chapter 2 I argued that a theory of sense as linguistic understanding is consistent with a Russell/Mill model of language on which referring expressions are directly referential. My point was that the Russell/Mill theorist could adopt a Fregean theory of sense (shorn of descriptivism about sense, and other features extraneous to the Fregean view, albeit not in the popular imagination) as a theory of understanding, while maintaining that the content of thought is a Russellian proposition, composed of individuals, properties, and so forth. It might be argued at this point, however, that the logical argument for the symmetry thesis smuggles in aspects of Fregeanism that are incompatible with the hybrid view sketched out earlier. Fregean thoughts are the bearers of truth and falsity, and so on Frege's view it follows that logical relations hold at the level of sense, not at the level of reference. But a Russell/Mill theorist might object that this goes beyond a Fregean theory of understanding. Even on the hybrid view, it might be objected, the bearers of truth and falsity are Russellian propositions, rather than Fregean senses. So logical relations between what sentences express need not have any consequences for how we think about sense.

A conciliatory response would concede the point about logic, while refocusing the discussion on the possibility of meaningful disagreement. Even if Russell/Mill propositions are the bearers of truth and falsehood, disagreement is a more fine-grained phenomenon that needs to be located at the level of sense. If both of us are unaware that Hesperus is Phosphorus, then we are not meaningfully disagreeing when you say "Hesperus is the morning star" and I say "Phosphorus is not the morning star," even though our two utterances cannot have the same truth value. In these circumstances I am not denying what you are saying. The point of the argument for the symmetry thesis, though, is that I can (in the right context) use "I" to deny what you have said using "you." So, denial is what is important, not difference of truth value.

This conciliatory response may concede too much, however. Most philosophical logicians understand the speech act of denial as the assertion of a negation.[9] If that is correct, then denial and

---

[9] This view goes back to Frege's essay 'Negation' (1918a), but is independent of his views about thoughts and senses. See Ripley 2011 for a review of current thinking

negation need to be understood on the same level. They cannot be separated as the conciliatory response proposes, but must be either both at the level of sense or at the level of reference. When the issue is formulated in terms of negation it is difficult not to beg the question. Is "Phosphorus is not the morning star" the negation of "Hesperus is the morning star"? Since the Russell/Mill theorist holds that the respective contents of these two sentences are <Venus, the property of being the morning star> and <Venus, the property of being the morning star, NOT> it is natural for them to claim that one sentence is indeed the negation of the other. A Fregean, on the other hand, is likely to point out, first, that a rational person who just happened to be ignorant of the Hesperus-Phosphorus identity could reasonably accept both sentences as true and then, second, that it ought to be apparent to a speaker in normal circumstances when one sentence differs from another only in negating what the other assets to be the case. A consistent Russell/Mill theorist will of course accept the datum and deny the intuition.

The issue seems much clearer when put in terms of denial rather than negation. Denial is a speech act and so taking into account the communicative intentions of the speaker is entirely appropriate. There may be contrived cases where it is acceptable to describe someone as denying something unknowingly, but the paradigm cases of denial are knowing speech acts. I know what you are saying and I intend what I say to contradict it. Here is how Smiley describes matters (using "rejection" where I use "denial"): "Where assertion expresses assent to a proposition, rejection expresses dissent from it, in each case by means of a sentence whose sense

---

about the relation between negation, denial, and rejection. There are very few philosophers who reject what Ripley terms the *denial equivalence* (i.e. the equivalence of denying p and asserting $\sim p$). Some are motivated by nonstandard views about negation. The denial equivalence cannot be accepted, for example, by someone who believes that both A and the negation of A can be true. For a different and very subtle motivation for rejecting the denial equivalence see Smiley 1996. There is nothing in this literature, as far as I can see, that challenges the basic point I am trying to make.

is the proposition in question."[10] Smiley's view is that denial is a speech act distinct from assertion. The majority view is that denying p is equivalent to asserting $\sim p$. Either way, however, one cannot deny p without uttering a sentence whose sense includes the sense of p. If there is a distinct speech act of denial then what is denied is simply p. Otherwise what is asserted is $\sim p$.

I turn now to an epistemological motivation for the symmetry thesis. The key driver here is that communication is a way of transmitting knowledge. In the right circumstances, my hearing you say something and understanding it gives me warrant to believe it and, when what you say is true, my belief can count as knowledge.[11] An essential part of what makes it possible for testimony to transmit warrant and/or knowledge is that what you say is what I come to know. To take an example, suppose I ask you "Where am I?" and you reply "You are in Miami, OH," what I learn through your utterance of "You are in Miami, OH" is exactly the knowledge that I would express through the sentence "I am in Miami, OH." This requires the token-equivalence of "I" and "you" in this conversational context. And so we have further support for the Symmetry Constraint.

The basic idea that acquiring knowledge through testimony requires the content of what is said to be the same as the content of the knowledge acquired is widely accepted.[12] But the examples given tend not to involve indexicals. For that reason I provide an

---

[10] Smiley 1996, p. 1.

[11] This seems a basic starting point in thinking about testimony as a source of knowledge. Compare the *default rule for testimony* suggested in Adler 2015: "If the speaker S asserts that p to the hearer H, then, under normal conditions, it is *correct* for H to *accept* (believe) S's assertion, unless H has special reason to object." As Adler observes, the default rule has suggested to many the following principle: "If S knows that p and S asserts that p to H, and H accepts p on the basis of S's testimony, then H knows that p." For further discussion see Jack 1993, McDowell 1993, Lackey 2008, and the essays in Lackey and Sosa 2006.

[12] It is explicit, for example, in the two generally accepted principles given in the previous footnote.

explicit argument for the identity claim. Suppose that there is no such token-equivalence. Then, assuming a standard, Fregean way of thinking about sameness and difference of what is said, my acceptance of what you say would be rationally cotenable with denying that I am in Miami, Ohio. But this cannot be reconciled with the thesis that, simply by virtue of hearing you say that I am in Miami, Ohio, I come to know that I am in Miami, Ohio. If it is rationally permissible for me to understand your utterance of "You are in Miami, Ohio" while at the same time denying that I am in Miami, Ohio, then my understanding your utterance cannot transmit testimony and/or knowledge.

In response to an earlier version of this argument Daniel Morgan objects that my argument for the Symmetry Constraint depends upon an unrealistic picture of how communication works. He thinks that I am committed to the following principle:

(U) Understanding a speaker's utterance requires thinking the very thought the speaker expresses in that utterance.[13]

As it happens I agree with Morgan that this is not a good model of linguistic communication—and also with Michael Dummett and Richard Heck who have also rejected the picture Morgan characterizes as (U) as a general requirement upon communication, both motivated by considerations of indexicals.[14] If genuine communication were really this demanding there would not be much of it about. What I do claim, however, is that knowledge through testimony typically requires the person acquiring the knowledge to think the very thought expressed by the speaker.

To motivate this further, consider Dummett's important distinction between thinking the same thought as someone else and knowing which thought that person expressed in their utterance.

[13] Morgan 2009, responding to Bermúdez 2005b.
[14] Dummett 1981 Ch. 6 and Heck 2002.

Where Frege took a false step was in arguing that communication must involve the hearer's thinking the very same thought as that voiced by the speaker, whereas all that is necessary is that he should attach the same significance to the words as the speaker does... Let us say that someone knows what thought was expressed by an utterance if he both grasps the significance of the words used and knows at least the minimum necessary for him to identify the referents of any indexicals occurring in the utterance.[15] (p. 127)

As an account of what is minimally required for communication to take place this is plausible enough. Certainly it would be hard to say that I have understood what you said if I either failed to grasp the significance of your words or lacked a means of identifying the referents of any indexicals that you used. But the issue is not what minimally has to hold for me to understand your utterance, but rather in virtue of what does my understanding your utterance give me knowledge of what you have said.

Everything depends upon what counts as the minimum necessary for me to identify the referents of any indexicals occurring in the utterance. Identifying the referent of an indexical requires thinking of somebody or something in a certain way. If I think about that person or thing in the same way that the speaker does then Dummett's account is not an alternative to the one I have proposed. So we need to consider the circumstance in which the speaker and I think about the referent(s) of the indexical(s) in different ways (under different modes of presentation). It seems to me that Dummett's proposal runs into a dilemma when we consider it in the light of Frege's criterion for distinctness of thoughts. Assume that what you say is true and you sincerely utter it for the purpose of communicating—a paradigm case for the transmission of knowledge through testimony. We need to ask: Does the way in which I identify the referent allow me to understand what you say and judge it to be false? If that is possible, then

---

[15] Dummett 1981, p. 127.

I don't seem to have acquired knowledge through understanding what you've said, because my beliefs would fail to be suitably sensitive to the truth value of your utterance.[16] But, on the other hand, if it is not possible then, by Frege's own criterion (which Dummett accepts), there seems to be no respect in which the thought that I am thinking can differ from the thought that you initially expressed.

Something that may be muddying the waters here is potential confusion with a similar case in which knowledge most definitely can be derived from testimony. Suppose that you hear Dummett say "I am hungry." Drawing on your background knowledge that it is Dummett who is speaking, that he is speaking sincerely, and so on, you can definitely acquire the knowledge that Dummett is hungry, and you will have acquired that knowledge through testimony. But this is certainly not a case in which what you come to know is what Dummett expressed, since Dummett expressed the thought that he himself is hungry, not the thought that Dummett is hungry. What we need, and what I will provide in later chapters, is an account of the sense of "I" in which what I come to know is what Dummett said, namely, that he himself is hungry.

4.3. Summary

Both Frege and Evans are committed to viewing the sense of "I" as a special way in which each individual is given to herself. Since this is not a way in which that person can be presented to anyone else, thoughts involving the sense of "I" cannot be grasped by anyone but that thinker. Evans bites the bullet and tries to argue that private "I"-thoughts can nonetheless be objective, capable of

---

[16] I am assuming here that knowledge tracks the truth in the sense suggested in Nozick 1981. In particular my belief that p counterfactually depends upon p, so that '$p \square\!\!\rightarrow Bp$' and '$\sim p \square\!\!\rightarrow \sim Bp$' are both true (where 'B' is the belief operator and '$\square\!\!\rightarrow$' the subjunctive conditional).

existing and having a truth value independently of any episode of thinking. As we saw in section 4.1, however, his arguments are ultimately unsuccessful. In section 4.2 I offered three lines of argument supporting what I termed the Symmetry Constraint, which holds that an account of the sense of "I" must allow tokens of "I" to have the same sense as tokens of other personal pronouns such as "you" in appropriate contexts. We need the Symmetry Constraint, I argued, in order to account for how indexical utterances can be reported; for how a speaker using one personal pronoun can deny what another speaker said using "I"; and for how understanding someone else's "I"-sentence can be a source of knowledge.

5
Token-Sense and Type-Sense

What I understand by your utterance of "you" in a given context is often exactly what you understand by my utterance of "I" in that same context. This gives:

The Symmetry Constraint
An account of the sense of "I" must allow tokens of "I" to have the same sense as tokens of other personal pronouns such as "you" in appropriate contexts.

The Symmetry Constraint has many interesting consequences. For one thing it immediately rules out any account of the sense of "I" on which "I"-thoughts are private and unshareable. So neither Frege's remarks nor Evans's more worked out account can be accepted as they stand.

Another consequence of the Symmetry Constraint is that we need to distinguish two different ways of thinking about sense—the token-sense of "I," on the one hand, and the type-sense of "I," on the other. The token-sense of "I" is what a speaker or hearer understands when they utter or hear an utterance involving "I." The type-sense of "I," on the other hand, is that by virtue of which a speaker or hearer can properly be said to understand the expression "I." Section 5.1 spells out the distinction between token-sense and type-sense in more detail, offering additional reasons for adopting the distinction. Section 5.2 compares the type-sense/token-sense distinction to other, more familiar distinctions from the discussion of indexicals, focusing in particular on Kaplan's distinction between character and content and Perry's distinction between content-C, content-D, and content-M.

5.1. Motivating the Distinction between Token-Sense and Type-Sense

It may be that for nonindexical expressions the notions of type-sense and token-sense coincide. But it is worth considering the possibility that they do not. The distinction may help clarify some issues that came up in the Chapter 2 discussion of what it is to understanding a proper name. Many theorists have been attracted to very minimal accounts of what it is to understand a proper name "ψ," on which it is enough simply to understand that "ψ" has the syntactic role of a proper name, together with mastery of the disquotational principle that "ψ" names ψ.[1] It certainly seems right at some level to say that I can understand an utterance of the sentence "ψ is F," even when I know nothing about ψ except that he or she has a name and is being said to be F. I would have no difficulty in continuing the conversation, for example, or reporting what has been said to a third party. On the other hand, such understanding would surely be very partial. It would give me very little grip on the sentence's semantic value. If I wanted to put myself in a position to determine whether the sentence is true or false, or even to know what would count as evidence for its being true or false, then I have to think about ψ in a more specific way (under a more specific mode of presentation). It may be helpful to think of this additional element in terms of the token-sense of the

[1] For references see Chapter 2, n. 25.

proper name "ψ," while the type-sense of "ψ" is what provides the minimal understanding of how "ψ" functions in English.

Be that as it may, the distinction between type-sense and token-sense is plainly called for in the case of indexicals. Understanding how the expression "I" functions in English is very different from understanding how the expression "you" functions, even though (as we have seen) the sense of "I" can be identical to the sense of "you" in appropriate contexts. The same holds for other pairs of indexicals such as "here" and "there"; "now" and "then"; or "this" and "that." In suitable contexts I can use "there" or "then" to deny what you say using "here" or "now." Consider the sentence:

(1) In the basement of her house on the morning of Monday, September 22, 2015 Mary said, "It's cold here now," but I happen to know that it was warm there then.

Here I express my understanding of what was said, making explicit enough of the context to anchor the indexicals, and then deny what I have just reported. This is exactly the sort of example that motivates the Symmetry Constraint. Here the words that I use in the denial share token-sense with the words in *oratione recta* that I am denying. But each member of the relevant pairs ("here" and "there"; "now" and "then") plays a very different linguistic role from the other. What I understand when I understand this particular use of "here" is the same as what I understand when I understand this particular use of "there," but of course in general what it is to understand "here" is very different from what it is to understand "there."

To make this basic thought more precise we need to look once more at the relation between understanding, sense, and truth conditions. As I have emphasized, at the most fundamental level to grasp a sense is to apprehend a truth condition. Grasping a sentence's truth condition is not to be equated, as some would have it, with being able to determine the sentence's truth value, or (a little more weakly) with knowing what would be involved in determining the sentence's truth value. Both of these views come too close to verificationism for comfort. Verificationism overemphasizes process over outcome. I can possess and apply a procedure for determining whether a number is prime without understanding what a prime number is. On the notion of understanding with which we are working, to understand a sentence is to know how the world would have to be for that sentence to be true, where (for example) this requires being able to recognize when the sentence's truth value has been determined. So, for example, in order to understand the sentence "83 is a prime number," I need to know enough of what a prime number is to be able to accept (or reject) a purported proof that 83 is indeed prime. Knowing that prime numbers are divisible only by themselves and by 1 is enough to be able to do that. I certainly don't need to have any inkling of an algorithm that I could apply to any number to tell me whether or not that number is prime. Still, I do need to know more than that the sentence "83 is a prime number is true" if and only if 83 is a prime number.

There are different ways in which one can know what it would be for a sentence to be true, as emerges particularly clearly in the case of indexicals. The Fregean, Russellian, and hybrid models of how sentences express thoughts all agree on the canonical form of a truth condition. For a sentence of the form "*a* is *F*" its truth condition is an ordered pair of an individual and a property—e.g. <*a*,—is *F*>. This is exactly what one would expect, given the disquotational truism that "*a* is *F*" is true if and only if *a* is *F*. Correlatively, we can think of the sense of "*a*" as a way of thinking about the individual that is *a* (as a mode of presentation of *a*), and the sense of "–is *F*" as a way of thinking about the property *F*(–). So, at a very abstract level, the sense of the sentence "*a* is *F*" is a way of thinking about the state of affairs of *a* being *F*.

Indexicals bring into focus the possibility of a different level at which a truth condition can be grasped. I can understand an indexical utterance even if I am not in any position to think about a specific individual. Imagine that I find a fragment of a newspaper article missing every means of identifying the author or the time/place of writing and I read the sentence "I repudiate the view I expressed yesterday that the rate of inflation in this country is higher today than officially reported." There is a sense in which I can understand this sentence perfectly well. Given that I have no information whatsoever about the context in which it was written I cannot in any substantive sense be said to be thinking about any specific individual repudiating on a certain day their previous day's view that the rate of inflation in their country is higher than officially reported. Nonetheless, in one sense I still know exactly what it would be for the sentence to be true—namely that the author of the sentence, on the day of writing, repudiates the view they expressed the previous day to the effect that the rate of inflation their country is higher than officially reported.

The distinction between type-sense and token-sense marks this distinction between two ways of grasping the truth condition of a sentence involving indexicals. The following makes the contrast explicit:

Grasping the *type-sense* of an indexical requires:

(a) being aware of how the referent of the indexical is determined by the context of utterance;
(b) knowing in general terms what it would be for the sentence featuring the indexical to be true (without necessarily being able to identify the referent of the indexical).

Grasping the *token-sense* of an indexical requires:

(a) being able to exploit features of the context of utterance to determine the referent of the indexical;
(b) knowing a specific truth condition (where this requires being able to identify the referents of the indexical).

So, in the case of "I," grasping the expression's type-sense is a matter of grasping that the referent of "I" is fixed by the token-reflexive view that a token of "I" refers to the utterer of that token, and hence of knowing that a token "I"-sentence is true just if the utterer of the sentence is as the sentence says she is. Grasping the token-sense of "I" is a matter of being able, relative to a specific utterance within a specific context, to exploit features of the context of utterance to determine to whom the token of "I" refers, and hence to be able to think of a particular state of affairs as the truth condition of the utterance.

Any account of sense that simultaneously ties the notion of sense to linguistic understanding and makes grasping a sense has to accommodate the palpable fact that linguistic understanding can occur with minimal levels of cognitive achievement (as illustrated by many of Kripke and Donnellan's famous examples).[2] A natural response would be to set the bar for linguistic understanding very low. But then we inevitably lose sight of what is distinctively going on in the nonminimal cases. If we have a unitary notion of understanding and look for a necessary condition on what it is to understand "I" that will capture all cases that can be described as understanding "I," even those where there is no knowledge of the relevant contextual features, then there is little prospect of shedding light upon the relation between "I"-sentences and "I"-thoughts, or the role that understanding "I" plays in self-conscious thought.

The distinction between type-sense and token-sense finesses this problem. The understanding that is undeniably there in what one might think of as the minimal cases (the newspaper article where the author and date are lost, or the exchange overheard when telephone lines are crossed) can be explained in terms of type-sense, leaving the notion of token-sense for the more canonical cases where, as it were, all the pieces are in place. While understanding any "I"-sentence requires, at a minimum, a grasp of the

[2] Burge has emphasized similar points in discussing Fregean sense in Burge 1979, 1990. Burge 2010 contains sustained attacks on "over-intellectualizing" basic representational capacities, primarily in the context of perception. I will return to his criticisms of Evans in Chapter 6.

type-sense of "I," the deep connections between the sense of "I" and self-conscious thought are to be found at the level of token-sense. As will emerge in Chapter 6, the token-sense of "I" is to be understood in terms of a set of locational abilities. Those abilities do not need to be exercised whenever a speaker uses "I" with understanding, or whenever a hearer understands someone else's use of "I"—because these might be occasions that involve nothing more than the type-sense of "I." Nonetheless, I will argue that one cannot deploy and engage the type-sense of "I" without at least possessing those abilities.

5.2. Comparisons

So how is the distinction between type-sense and token-sense related to some of the other important distinctions that have emerged in thinking about indexicals? Kaplan's two-way distinction between character and content and to Perry's three-way distinction between content-M, content-C, and content-D were both formulated specifically to accommodate indexicals.[3] However, there is no way of applying either of them to map onto the distinction between type-sense and token-sense. What causes difficulty is the need, at the level of token-sense, to do justice both to Frege's criterion for the sameness/distinctness of senses and to the Symmetry Constraint.

Kaplan's influential distinction between character and content is one of the pillars of the Russell/Mill view of language discussed in Chapter 2. Kaplan's distinction can be characterized either formally or informally. From a formal point of view, the distinction needs to be understood against the background of Kaplan's logic of demonstratives, itself formulated within a possible worlds framework. Nathan Salmon uses the useful terminology of information value

[3] Kaplan 1989 and Perry 1997.

to summarize the basic picture.[4] The information value of a sentence is the information it encodes, a function of the information values of its subsentential constituent and their mode of combination. The information value of any expression is a semantic intension, that is, a function that assigns to a world w the extension that a singular term, sentence, or predicate takes in that world. The extension of a singular term at a world is its referent at that world; of a sentence its truth value; and of a predicate the class of n-tuples to which the predicate applies. For Kaplan the content of a sentence (the thought that it expresses) is fixed by the extensions of its subsentential constituents. It is a Russell/Mill proposition, composed of individuals, properties, and so forth.

For Kaplan indexicals are directly referential, just like other naming expressions. What they contribute to the content of sentences containing them is simply the individual that they pick out. But, because indexicals are context-sensitive, bringing them within his general framework requires relativizing an expression's information value/semantic intension to the context in which it is uttered. Indexical expressions can have different information values at different contexts of utterance. And so for indexicals Kaplan introduces a new notion. The character of an indexical expression is a function from contexts of utterance to information values. The information value of "I" at a given context is a function from contexts of utterance to a function that in every possible world picks out the agent of that context.[5]

In "Demonstratives" Kaplan tends (more informally) to equate the character of "I" with its linguistic meaning, offering the following three principles as giving the character of "I":

---

[4] See Salmon 1989, section 1.

[5] So, the character of "I" is a function from contexts to another function—not from contexts to the agent of that context. Salmon introduces the helpful terminology of an expression's *contour* to capture the function from context to the referent of the expression in the context. As he notes (1989, p. 334) the contour of "I" is fully determined by its character.

Token-Sense and Type-Sense ~ 87

(D1) "I" is an indexical, different utterances of which may have different contents.
(D2) "I" is, in each of its utterances, directly referential.
(D3) In each of its utterances, "I" refers to the person who utters it.[6]

Kaplan emphasizes that character applies to words and phrases as types.[7] And it seems to function rather similarly to type-sense as we have developed it. If someone knows the type-sense of "I," together with enough details of the context to enable the reference-fixing rule to be applied, then she is in a position to determine the reference of the token utterance of "I" and with it the content of the utterance. An initial proposal, then, is that we simply identify type-sense with what Kaplan calls character and token-sense with what he terms content.

This proposal plainly satisfies the Symmetry Constraint. Relative to a particular context, the content fixed by my use of "I" is exactly the same as the content fixed by your use of "you." Both utterances share a single truth condition and, for Kaplan, that truth condition is their content. A comparable equation of token-sense and content would have the same desirable consequence for the other pairs of indexicals we have discussed.

But the notion of token-sense is supposed to be correlative with the notion of understanding, and the notion of content (in Kaplan's sense) is too coarse-grained to do the job required. Suppose that "I" corefers with the proper name "ψ." Then, in the appropriate context, there is no difference in content between the sentences "I am F" and "ψ is F." But there is generally an important gap between understanding these two sentences. This is the indisputable upshot of discussions of essential indexicals, as recapitulated and extended in Chapter 1. Nor is the difference between understanding "I am F" and "ψ is F" confined to contexts of action and psychological explanation. It is also reflected in the twin facts (a) that "ψ is F"

---

[6] Kaplan 1989, p. 520.   [7] Ibid., p. 524.

cannot generally be embedded in reports of "I am F" and (b) that "ψ is not F" is not in general immediately understood as a denial of "I am F," even holding the context constant. It is not hard to imagine contexts in which I am addressing ψ but where I am unaware that her name is "ψ," and so fail to take a third party's utterance of "ψ is not F" to be the denial of ψ's own assertion "I am F." But this difference between understanding "I am F" and understanding "ψ is F" is precisely what the notion of token-sense is being called upon to explain. So, equating token-sense with Kaplan's content and type-sense with Kaplan's character fails to line up in the right way with Frege's criterion of identity/distinctness for senses (although it does satisfy the Symmetry Constraint).

Perhaps it was a mistake to locate token-sense at the level of content? Kaplan emphasizes that his notion of character applies to expression-types, rather than to expression-tokens, and he emphasizes that all referring expressions, including indexicals, are directly referential. At the same time, though, he explicitly holds that objects are apprehended under modes of presentation and, in fact, he explicitly states that "a character may be likened to a mode of presentation of an object."[8] In section XVII of "Demonstratives" Kaplan applies this general picture to the first person pronoun, proposing that the cognitive significance of an utterance involving "I" be understood in terms of the character of "I."

What is the particular and primitive way in which Dr Lauben is presented to himself? What cognitive content presents Dr Lauben to himself, but presents him to nobody else? Thought determined this way can be grasped by Dr Lauben, but no one else can grasp *that* thought determined in *that* way. The answer, I believe, is, simply, that Dr Lauben is presented to himself under the character of "I".[9]

This suggests a second way of interpreting the type-sense/token-sense distinction. As before, we can equate type-sense with the

---

[8] Ibid., p. 533.   [9] Ibid., p. 533.

notion of character viewed as a model of the conventional linguistic meaning of "I" (what a competent language-user needs to know in order to use and understand the first person pronoun). The notion of token-sense is also captured through the notion of character, but here it is character considered as mode of presentation. Kaplan's suggestion, if I understand it correctly, is that the utterer of "I" thinks of himself as the person who is referring to himself through uttering "I"—and, by the same token, someone else hearing me utter a sentence including "I" will think of me as the person who is referring to himself through uttering "I."

Interpreting token-sense through character in this way clearly avoids the problems with Frege's criterion of sameness/distinctness for senses that come with equating token-sense with Kaplan's content. If "I" is understood in terms of a character-like mode of presentation of the utterer to herself then there is no danger of failing to mark the distinction between "I am F" and "ψ is F." However, this second proposal has real difficulties accommodating the Symmetry Constraint.

One problem is that the character of "I" is completely different from the character of "you," whereas the Symmetry Constraint demands that the token-sense of "I" be equivalent to the token-sense of "you," modulo a given context. If the token-sense of my utterance of "I" is given by my thinking of myself under the mode of presentation *person currently referring to himself through uttering "I"* and the token-sense of your utterance of "you" is given by your thinking of me under the mode of presentation *person currently being referred to by my utterance of "you"* then your utterance of "you are not F" cannot count as a denial of my utterance of "I am F," as discussed in Chapter 4. This point, were it the only difficulty, could be finessed, however. It is fairly easy to map the character of "I" onto the character of "you" in a way that might be thought sufficient for the Symmetry Constraint. If I am addressing you then, in virtue of giving a rule for determining the referent of "I" as the utterer of the relevant token of "I," the character of "I" to all intents and purposes fixes the referent of "you" (as the person whom *this* person, the utterer of "I," is addressing).

But there is a more serious problem. A character-based notion of mode of presentation is just too weak to do one of the important jobs for which we need the distinction between type-sense and token-sense. One thing that we want the notion of token-sense to do is distinguish the way in which I understand what I read when I stumble across a piece of paper in the street on which all that remains legible is the first line of a will ("I write this document in full possession of my faculties...") from the way in which I understand those very same words when I am present on an occasion when the will is being read. I suggested that minimal cases of understanding such as this one (in which the relevant details of the context are not available) can be accommodated at the level of type-sense, leaving token-sense for the cases of understanding where speaker and/or hearer are aware of how contextual parameters have been set. The difficulty with the current proposal, however, is that all the requirements it places on grasping the token-sense of "I" are satisfied in minimal cases, such as encountering the fragmented will. When I come across the piece of paper I am perfectly capable of thinking about the author of the will under the mode of presentation *the person referring to himself through this inscription of "I."* So, from the perspective of a character-based interpretation of mode of presentation, there is no relevant difference between the minimal case and the nonminimal case. Both the inscription and the utterance of "I write this document..." exploit the reference-fixing rule given by the character of "I" and I apply that rule to think about the author of the will in exactly the same way when I read the piece of paper by an unknown author as when I hear the lawyer read out the words written by a familiar hand.

There are different ways of understanding an utterance's truth conditions. It is agreed on (almost) all sides that we understand an utterance by grasping its truth condition (by understanding how the world would have to be for that utterance to be true). But I can understand the truth condition of an utterance in a way that does not put me in any position to know how to go about establishing whether or not that condition holds. This is exactly what is happening in the first case. I know, in what one might think of as an abstract sense, what it would be for the inscription to be true. It is true just if the writer was in full possession of his faculties at the time of writing. But, not knowing who the writer is or how to go about identifying him, let alone the time of utterance, I am not in a position to make any progress in determining the utterance's truth value. This level of understanding contrasts with a practical grasp of an utterance's truth condition, where this would put one in a position to determine the utterance's truth value, or at least to be able to recognize what would count as evidence for assigning a particular truth value.

This idea that there are different levels in understanding truth conditions, particularly for utterances involving indexicals, has been taken up and developed by John Perry. Perry has proposed for indexical expressions a distinction between different types of content intended to be more fine-grained than Kaplan's distinction between character and content.[10] Whereas Kaplan simply distinguishes content from character, Perry distinguishes between what he calls content-M (more or less corresponding to Kaplan's character) and two additional notions of content, content-C and content-D, that between them do the work of Kaplan's content. Strikingly, he supports his three-way taxonomy with considerations from same-saying not unlike those raised earlier in this paper.

The twin ideas behind Perry's taxonomy are, first, that content is given in terms of truth conditions and, second, that truth conditions are assessed relative to a set of background facts taken as fixed. The three types of content differ in which background facts are taken as fixed. The most general type of content is content-M, which corresponds to the truth conditions of the utterance given

[10] See Perry 1997.

the basic syntactic and semantic facts about the utterance. So, for example, the truth condition in content-M terms of my utterance "I am now in the best university in Texas" is roughly speaking that the utterer of the token sentence is, at the time of uttering it, in the best university in Texas. The next most determinate type of content is content-C, corresponding to the truth conditions relative to the relevant contextual information required to fix the reference of the indexical expressions. The content-C truth conditions are that JLB is in the best university in Texas on the morning of Monday, September 28, 2015. Finally, the content-D of an utterance corresponds to the truth conditions relative to all of the above information, in addition to whatever information is required to fix the reference of other expressions. The only additional information required to specify the content-D of my utterance is to identify a particular university as the best university in Texas.

Perry's taxonomy can be characterized in the following way. The content-M of a typical indexical utterance of the form "I am F," where F includes a descriptive component, is a singular proposition about the utterance itself, while content-C and content-D are both singular propositions whose subject is the referent of "I." In the case of content C the singular proposition retains an element whose referent remains unspecified. The omission is remedied in content-D. Content-D corresponds to Kaplan's notion of content. It is a Russell/Mill proposition.

According to Perry, the cognitively relevant content of an indexical utterance is content-M, while Content-D is a complete characterization of the utterance's truth condition. What he terms the "official" content is given by content-C, where the official content of an utterance is what it says. In this respect he departs from Kaplan, for whom official content is what Perry calls content-D.[11]

---

[11] But Perry remains consistent with the two-level view of content laid out in Perry 1977, 1979. Content-M corresponds to belief-state (1979) and sense (1977),

One of Perry's two arguments for locating official content at the level of content-C is what he calls the same-saying argument. Content-C is official content, Perry maintains, because it allows for utterances of "I am F" and "you are F" to say the same thing in an appropriate context. In so doing, of course, the notion of content-C satisfies the Symmetry Constraint. But the problem, as with Kaplan's notion of content, is that the price is too high. The content-C common to "I am F" and "you are F" is also shared with "ψ is F," where "ψ" corefers with "I" and "you." In fact, Perry sees this as an advantage of the notion of content-C. Here is how Perry puts the same-saying argument.

Consider my utterance, directed at my son Jim:

(14) You were born in Lincoln

The content-M of (14) is a proposition about (14). But we would ordinarily count me as having said the same thing to him as he said to me with his utterance:

(15) I was born in Lincoln.

And the same thing I say to a third party with my utterance:

(1) Jim was born in Lincoln.

But these two utterances have quite different contents-M than (14). The content-M of (15) is a proposition about (15) itself, and the content-M of (1) is just a singular proposition about Jim (since names name, their designation is fixed by their meaning). It seems, then, that it is the individual designated by the sub-utterance of "you," and not the condition of being the addressee of that sub-utterance, that makes it into the official content of (14).[12]

---

while content-C corresponds to belief (1979) and thought (1977). So his taxonomy here is really an extension rather than a revision of the earlier discussion.

[12] Perry 1997, p. 603.

But this is not quite right. The Symmetry Constraint holds that it must be *possible* for "I"-utterances and "you"-utterances to say the same thing—and, moreover, in the right circumstances, it must be possible for "I"-utterances, "you"-utterances, and, in some circumstances, "ψ"-utterances (where "ψ" is a proper name) that predicate the same property of the same person to say the same thing. But the Symmetry Constraint is a modal constraint and it has to leave open the possibility that these three different token utterances do not say the same thing, even when the referring expressions all pick out the same person. This would not be possible on Perry's account of official content. On his notion of content-C, a token "I"-utterance, a token "you"-utterance, and a token "ψ"-utterance that predicate the same property of the same person will automatically say the same thing. But then we will not be able to do justice to Frege's criterion of sameness/difference for thoughts, because there will certainly be contexts where I might affirm "I am F" but deny "ψ is F"—contexts that Perry himself has worked hard to draw to our attention.

There certainly is, according to Perry, a level of content at which "I am F" and "ψ is F" have different contents. This is the level of content-M. But, since content-M is essentially Kaplan's notion of character, we encounter again the same difficulty that we encountered with the first proposal. At the level at which "I am F" and "ψ is F" say different things, "I am F" and "you are F" also have to say different things (even in the type of contexts we have been discussing). So we lose touch with the Symmetry Constraint.

5.3. Summary

The Symmetry Constraint holds that an account of the sense of "I" must allow tokens of "I" to have the same sense as tokens of other personal pronouns such as "you" in appropriate contexts. Since there is an obvious sense in which understanding "I" is fundamentally different from understanding "you" (and "he") this means that we need to distinguish two forms of sense—one applicable to token utterances (token-sense) and one applicable to utterance-types (type-sense). Here is the general distinction.

Grasping the *type-sense* of an indexical requires:

(a) being aware of how the referent of the indexical is determined by the context of utterance;

(b) knowing in general terms what it would be for the sentence featuring the indexical to be true (without necessarily being able to identify the referent of the indexical);

Grasping the *token-sense* of an indexical requires:

(a) being able to exploit features of the context of utterance to determine the referent of the indexical;

(b) knowing a specific truth condition (where this requires being able to identify the referents of the indexical).

Section 5.2 looked at how the type-sense/token-sense distinction differs from other distinctions developed in the context of indexicals by David Kaplan and John Perry. The key point is that a satisfactory account of token-sense must simultaneously do two things. First, it must respect the Symmetry Constraint (including the fact that it is a modal constraint, allowing for appropriately coreferring "I"-utterances and "you"–utterances to say the same thing, but not making it automatic). Second, it must respect Frege's criterion for sameness/difference of sense (particularly with respect to coreferential proper names). All of the proposals that we considered failed on at least one of these dimensions. Chapter 6 develops a model of the type-sense and token-sense of "I" that meets both of these requirements.

6
"I": Token-Sense and Type-Sense

The discussion so far has revealed five constraints that any satisfactory account of the token-sense and type-sense of "I" must satisfy. The first emerged from the discussion of essential indexicality in Chapter 1.

Constraint 1 (Essential Indexicality)
Explain the distinctive cognitive role of "I"-thoughts, as reflected in the two principles Essential Indexicality (Agency) and Essential Indexicality (Explanation).

Chapter 4 showed that private "I"-thoughts cannot be objective. So, anyone committed to holding that "I"-thoughts can be objective must believe that they are shareable.

Constraint 2 (Shareability)
Allow thoughts containing the sense of "I" to be shareable.

Shareability in turn requires that there be contexts when the same thought can be expressed by you using "you" and by me using "I." Hence:

Constraint 3 (Symmetry)
Allow tokens of "I" to have the same sense as tokens of other personal pronouns such as "you" in appropriate contexts.

The Symmetry Constraint is a modal constraint. It does not (and should not) require that tokens of "I" should always have the same sense as tokens of "you." Identity of sense holds only in certain contexts, circumscribed by Frege's criterion for sameness/distinctness of sense.

Constraint 4 (Frege's Criterion)
Individuate senses in accordance with Frege's criterion, so that no two token-senses can be the same if it is possible for a rational thinker to take incompatible attitudes to them.

There is a close connection between grasping the sense of a sentence (a thought) and apprehending the truth condition of that sentence/thought but, in the case of indexicals in general and "I" in particular, there are two ways of apprehending a truth condition.

Constraint 5 (Truth Conditions)
Accommodate the distinction between knowing in general terms what it would be for the sentence featuring the indexical to be true (without necessarily being able to identify the referent of the indexical) and knowing a specific truth condition (where this requires being able to identify the referents of the indexical).

The basic distinction between type-sense and token-sense is primarily motivated by Symmetry and Truth Conditions. The Symmetry Constraint is met at the level of token-sense, while the palpable differences between understanding "I" and understanding "you" are accommodated at the level of type-sense. Likewise the general understanding of what it would be for a sentence involving "I" to be true is a function of the type-sense of "I," while grasping the token-sense of "I" is required to apprehend the full truth condition of an "I"-sentence.

But that merely tells us that we need a distinction between type-sense and token-sense. It does not yet tell us how to develop each of those notions. This chapter offer a substantive account of the token-sense of "I." The account is presented in section 6.1, while section 6.2 spells out how it meets the five constraints. Section 6.3 turns to the type-sense of "I," following through on the earlier claim that the type-sense/token-sense distinction allows for different levels of understanding of "I" and making explicit some of the connections between self-reference and self-awareness implied by the account of the sense of "I."

6.1. The Token-Sense of "I"

Applying to the first person pronoun the general characterization of token-sense from Chapter 5 we see that grasping the token-sense of "I" relative to a particular context of utterance requires:

(a) being able to exploit features of the context of utterance to determine the reference of the indexical;
(b) knowing a specific truth condition (where this requires being able to identify the referents of the indexical).

At the same time, the general model of sense developed in Chapter 2 understands the sense of a referring expression as a way of thinking about the object to which the expression refers (a mode of presentation of that object). In the case of "I," of course, the object referred to is the speaker. So, putting these two ideas together, the token-sense of "I" must be a mode of presentation of the speaker to himself that allows features of the context to fix the reference of "I," thereby allowing either utterer or hearer to come to know a specific condition for the truth of the utterance. But how should we understand that mode of presentation?

For indexicals in general, and "I" in particular, the type/token distinction applies to ways of thinking of an object, as observed by Christopher Peacocke:

> The first distinction that we need is between type and token modes of presentation (ways of thinking) of something. Everyone who thinks a thought of the form "I am thus-and-so" thinks of himself in the same type of way: the type of the modes of presentation ("m.p.'s") in their various thoughts are identical, but in this special case there are exactly as many token m.p.'s of this type in their thoughts as there are people thinking the thoughts. The token m.p., not the type, must be the constituent of the thought if the thought is to play Frege's role (b) [viz. being the bearer of truth or falsity]: for the different token m.p.'s of a given type determine distinct objects. But those token m.p.'s should not be thought of as analogous to token expressions, particular utterances, or inscriptions. John's thought that he was born in 1950 is something to which he can take different attitudes at different times: in this sense the thought, though containing token m.p.'s, is repeatable.[1]

Two points. First, Peacocke's distinction between type modes of presentation and token modes of presentation does *not* map onto the distinction between type-sense and token-sense, as I have drawn it. The type-sense of an expression is not a mode of presentation of an object. Type-sense is much closer to the conventional linguistic meaning of the indexical expression.[2] Peacocke's distinction falls within the general category of token-sense. Second, as Peacocke notes, different token utterances can express a single token mode of presentation. So a token-sense is not an unrepeatable entity like a token utterance. He makes the point in the context of the same person thinking the same (token) thought at

---

[1] Peacocke 1981, p. 189.
[2] Compare Peacocke's remarks on why his distinction between type and token m.p.s cannot be assimilated to Kaplan's distinction between character and content: "Character is essentially linguistic, a rule for determining an object as referent of an expression from a context of utterance, whereas it is not excluded by the structure of the present account that someone should employ token m.p.'s in his thought while having no word in his language (if any) to express those mp.'s" (1981, p. 195).

different times, but (as we noted in discussing the Symmetry Constraint) we can have different people thinking the same thought, even in the case of "I"-thoughts.

Peacocke interprets token modes of presentation of "I" as type m.p.s indexed to objects. As he puts it, everyone who thinks "I am F" thinks of themselves under a common (type) mode of presentation—the type *self*. The distinct and unique thought that each person thinks is given by indexing the type *self* to the person thinking the thought. For thinker a Peacocke designates this token sense of "I" as [*self*$_a$], where the square brackets mark an indexing functor applied to the mode of presentation *self* and the thinker a. The same general model can be applied to the sense of "you." Here we have a (type) mode of presentation *you* that is indexed to the addressee of the utterance. So, in the kind of case motivating the Symmetry Constraint, where a is engaging with b and b is denying what a says, the token-sense of a's use of "I" is [*self*$_a$] and the token-sense of b's use of "you" is [*you*$_a$].

The vocabulary and machinery of indexing is not, as Peacocke emphasizes, a substantive account of the sense of any indexical. In his vocabulary a substantive account will specify, for each thinker t, object a, and indexical m.p. Δ, the relation R(Δ) in which t needs to stand to a in order to think about a under the m.p. Δ. In the case of the token-sense of "I," of course, $t = a$. So what we need is an account of the relation R(*self*) in which a needs to stand to a in order to think about a under the indexed mode of presentation [*self*$_a$]. Any account of the relation R(*self*) needs to respect the five constraints with which we began this chapter.

Frege's proposal, which he leaves undeveloped, is that "everyone is presented to himself in a special and primitive way, in which he is presented to no one else." Evans glosses this with an account of the sense of "I" that has three components:

Input component
"I"–thinkers are sensitive to sources of information about themselves that are immune to error though misidentification,

thereby allowing them to think thoughts about themselves that are identification-free.

Output component
"I"–thinkers are sensitive to the immediate implications for action of self-specifying information.

Objectivity component
"I"–thinkers are able to think of themselves from a third-person point of view, as elements in the objective order of things.

For Evans, then, R(*self*) is a complex of three sets of abilities—abilities to form judgments in response to certain types of information; abilities to act directly on certain types of information; and abilities to conceptualize oneself from an objective point of view. For *a* to think about *a* under the mode of presentation *self* is for *a* to exploit some or all of those abilities with respect to himself.

However, Evans is committed to the privacy and unshareability of the sense of "I" and hence of "I"-thoughts. This contravenes both the general Shareability Constraint and the more specific Symmetry Constraint. The first component of Evans's account is the most problematic. By tying the sense of "I" to sensitivity to types of information that are in principle inaccessible to anyone but the thinker, the input component effectively rules out the sense of "I," thus understood, being shared—and certainly makes it inconceivable that it might in the right circumstances be token-equivalent to the sense of "you" or any other personal pronoun.

Symmetry is more powerful in this context than Shareability. Peacocke proposes a strategy that might defuse concerns about Shareability, considered in isolation.

Unlike Evans, however, I hold that this apparatus is defensible only if we distinguish between *employing* a mode of presentation and *referring to* a mode of presentation. "[*self*$_{John}$]" cannot have as its sense that distinctive token m.p. under which only John and no one else can think of himself: if it were to have such a sense then sentences containing it could be understood only by John. "[*self*$_{John}$]" rather refers to that m.p. which can be a constituent only of John's, and no one else's, thoughts. From the fact that only John can think thoughts containing this m.p. it does not follow that we cannot know which thought he thinks, or that we cannot think about the constituent m.p.'s of his thoughts.[3]

Developing this idea further would require explaining how we can know which thought someone thinks when that thought is of a kind that in principle we cannot think. As we saw in Chapter 4, Dummett (who emphasizes a comparable distinction) offers such an explanation. This strategy may allay concerns about Shareability, if a shareable thought is understood as one that can be reported and discussed. However, as we observed in Chapter 4, the strategy is plainly incompatible with the possibility that a token of "I" share a sense with a token of "you." And for that very reason it cannot do justice to the motivations for adopting Symmetry, in particular the need to account for how knowledge can be acquired through testimony.

So, an account of the sense of "I" cannot include anything corresponding to Evans's input component. This creates a problem. We still need to account for the distinctive sense of first person utterances that are grounded in "private" information-sources such as introspection, somatic proprioception, and autobiographical memory, but we can no longer do so through the sense of "I." We will turn to this problem in Chapter 7.

What about the output component? Evans understands this in terms of the distinctive functional role of "I"-thoughts and the "I"-sentences that express them. Does this functional role account also run foul of Symmetry and Shareability? Daniel Morgan thinks so.

I stand in an input relationship to myself in which no one else stands: for example, only I receive proprioceptive information about myself (of course, other people stand in a corresponding privileged relationship

---

[3] Peacocke 1981, p. 191.

to themselves). I also stand in an output relationship to myself in which no one else stands: only I am capable of directly determining what my actions are to be (of course, other people stand in a corresponding privileged relationship to their actions). Any functional role account of "I"-thoughts will write one or other or both of these privileged relationships into the identity of an "I"-thought. For example, the idea might be that a thought is not identical with my thought that I am being pursued by a bear unless it feeds directly into my actions. Or the idea might be that a thought is not identical with my thought that I am cold unless it is directly sensitive to my way of gaining information about my own temperature. But it is clear that no thought that anyone else can entertain is going to be directly sensitive to my way of gaining information about my temperature, and no thought that any one else can entertain is going to feed directly into my actions. Hence a functional role account of "I"-thoughts entails that "I"-thoughts are unshareable.[4]

Morgan's is right to hold that, if the identity of a thought were dependent upon sensitivity to certain types of information that only I can experience, then that thought would certainly not be shareable. Chapter 7 will show that the significance and cognitive role of distinctively private information sources can be accommodated without making them constitutive of the identity of thoughts to which they give rise. In any event, though, there is an asymmetry between the input and output components here. We can (and should!) allow that the immediate implications for action of "I"-thoughts are constitutive of the identity of those thoughts without that making those thoughts unshareable.

To see how this works we need to look more carefully at what exactly is involved in the output component. Morgan proposes the following:

(1) A thought is not identical with my thought that I am being pursued by a bear unless it feeds directly into my actions.

---

[4] Morgan 2009, pp. 73–4.

(2) No thought that anyone else can entertain is going to feed directly into my actions.

I take issue with the formulation in (1), which effectively makes the denial of Shareability and Symmetry a matter of definition. The real issue, as noted in discussing Perry's comments about psychological explanation in section 3.1, is not who is performing the action, but what the goal of the action is. What matters for the thought that I myself am being pursued by a bear is that it should give rise to actions with the aim of extricating me from my predicament. Those might be actions that I perform—standing my ground and making noise (recommended), or running away (not recommended). Or they might be actions that someone else could perform—distracting the bear or attacking it with bear spray. So (1) needs to be reformulated along the lines of:

(1) A thought is not identical with my thought that I am being pursued by a bear unless it feeds directly into actions appropriately directed at me (e.g. saving me from the bear).

If I am entertaining the thought then obviously it will be me performing those actions. But someone else can entertain that very thought and perform actions with the same intended goal. For that reason (2) is false. It is certainly true that a thought can only feed directly into the actions of the person thinking it, but when we think about actions in terms of their intended goals then we see that someone else can think and act upon the same thought that I would express using "I." This would be a case, in Peacocke's terminology, of two token, indexed m.p.s ($[self_A]$ and $[he_A]$) that have the same functional role and indeed share a single token-sense.

So, incorporating the output component into an account of the token-sense of "I" does not contravene either Shareability or Symmetry. And plainly it accommodates Essential Indexicality. But do we need it? Could the speaker's/thinker's ability to act directly upon certain types of self-relevant information be due to more fundamental abilities? We need to ask: What is the distinctive information communicated by "I"-sentences and apprehended in "I"-thoughts? Following Perry and others we can frame this question in terms of the informational difference between the thought that JLB would express with the words "I am F" and the thought I might express with the words "JLB is F." These two thoughts have very different functional roles—that much is familiar. But to what informational differences does that difference in functional role correspond?

It is widely accepted that the thought expressed by "I am F" conveys self-locating information in a way that the thought expressed by "JLB is F" does not.[5] David Lewis's famous example of the two gods makes vivid the informational contribution of self-locating beliefs.

Consider the case of the two gods. They inhabit a certain possible world and they know exactly which world it is. Therefore they know every proposition that is true in their world. Insofar as knowledge is a propositional attitude, they are omniscient. Still I can imagine them to suffer ignorance: neither one knows which of the two he is. They are not exactly alike. One lives on top of the tallest mountain and throws down manna; the other lives on the top of the coldest mountain and throws down thunderbolts. Neither one knows whether he lives on the tallest mountain or on the coldest mountain; nor whether he throws down manna or thunderbolts.[6]

People sometimes wonder, confronted with this example, why each god cannot simply look at their own actions and use that to identify themselves—in effect, asking the question "Am I throwing

---

[5] Perry 1979 uses the expression "locating beliefs" to describe the thoughts expressed through indexical utterances. The terminology of "self-locating" is now standard, however. See Titelbaum 2008 and Bradley 2012, for example. Both papers discuss the interesting problem of how Bayesian models of confirmation and belief revision can accommodate self-locating beliefs.

[6] Lewis 1979, p. 139.

down mannah or throwing down thunderbolts?" Lewis's point, I take it, is that since they are gods they do not have any partial knowledge of that type. In fact, they cannot even ask the question. Their knowledge is all *sub specie aeternitatis*, composed of eternal propositions, free of indexicals and other signs of limitation. For the rest of us, however, self-location is everything. And in particular, as Perry emphasized in his articles on the subject, self-location is at the heart of essential indexicality. Why does the thought "I am about to be eaten by a bear" lead me to take evasive action? Because it records my location directly in the path of a hungry bear.

This suggests that the output component of the functional role of "I"-thoughts is *not* basic. What underlies the ability to act on certain types of self-relevant information is the ability to locate oneself within the world. Lewis's two gods have all the self-relevant information that there could be (*sub specie aeternitatis*), if only they were able to anchor that information by locating themselves within the world. We, on the other hand, are cursed with the opposite problem—the capacity for self-location combined with highly limited knowledge of self-relevant information.

For this reason Evans was wrong to separate out the output component of the sense of "I" from what I have termed the objectivity component. The objectivity component is really what is fundamental, because it underwrites the capacities for self-location that underlie the capacity to act upon self-relevant information. Consider again the passage where Evans introduces the objectivity component:

Indispensable though these familiar ingredients (an information component and an action component) are in any account of the Ideas we have of ourselves, . . . they cannot constitute an exhaustive account of our "I"-ideas. So long as we focus on judgments which a person might make about himself on the basis of the relevant ways of gaining knowledge, the inadequacy may not strike us. A subject's knowledge of what it is for the thought "I am in pain" to be true may appear to be exhausted by his capacity to decide, simply upon the basis of how he feels, whether or not it is true—and similarly in the case of all the other ways of gaining knowledge about ourselves. However, our view of ourselves is not Idealistic: we are perfectly capable of grasping propositions about ourselves which we are quite incapable of deciding, or even offering grounds for. I can grasp the thought that I was breast-fed, for example, or that I was unhappy on my first birthday, or that I tossed and turned in my sleep last night, or that I shall be dragged unconscious through the streets of Chicago, or that I shall die.   (Evans 1982, 208–9)

In judgments of the form "I am F" with the IEM property there is no gap between determining the presence of F-ness and determining that one is oneself F. But we can entertain many thoughts about ourselves that are not like that—thoughts about our distant past, for example, or about our future. These thoughts concern states of affairs whose holding or otherwise cannot be determined by us on the basis of information channels with the IEM property. In order to think such thoughts the subject must be able to think of himself in a much richer way than is required in order to grasp the truth condition of sentences that are immune to error through misidentification.

Since this class of "I"-houghts does not have the IEM property, we need a different account of how thinkers of such thoughts can have the relevant discriminating knowledge of themselves. For Evans this knowledge is to be understood in terms of subjects' ability to locate themselves within the objective spatio-temporal world.

It seems to me clear that as we conceive of persons, they are distinguished from one another by fundamental grounds of difference of the same kind as those which distinguish other physical things, and that a fundamental identification of a person involves a consideration of him as the person occupying such-and-such a spatio-temporal location. Consequently, to know what it is for $[\delta = I]$ to be true, for arbitrary δ, is to know what is involved in locating oneself in a spatio-temporal map of the world.   (Evans 1982, 211)

For Evans, being able to locate oneself within the objective spatio-world is a nontrivial achievement. It requires being able to integrate the egocentric space within which one acts with a non-egocentric, third-personal representation of space. It is, in short, a matter of possessing, and being able to situate oneself within what psychologists term a cognitive map of the world.[7]

Evans thinks that this ability is a third component in the sense of "I," complementing the two functional role dimensions that we have already discussed. My proposal, in contrast, is that this is all that we need. To grasp the token-sense of "I" is to think of oneself in a certain way (under the mode of presentation *self*). When one is thinking of oneself under the mode of presentation *self* one is thinking of oneself as an element in the objective spatiotemporal world, where this in turn typically requires being able to take the kind of external perspective on oneself manifested in locating oneself relative to a cognitive map of the world.

This proposal may seem unsatisfying. There is a vast experimental literature on cognitive maps in insects and nonhuman animals.[8] It seems very likely that the ability to navigate within a non-egocentric (allocentric) coordinate frame is phylogenetically far more primitive than any capacity for linguistic self-reference or self-conscious thought. So, one might ask, how can an account of self-reference and self-conscious thought be based on a navigational ability that seems to be enjoyed by cognitive unsophisticated creatures?

The answer is that locating oneself objectively relative to a cognitive map is very different from being able to deploy a cognitive map in spatial reasoning. In his extended discussion of Strawson and Evans in *Origins of Objectivity* Burge has made an important distinction that is very relevant here. He distinguishes between two

---

[7] This aspect of Evans's view has been taken up by Campbell 1994, Cassam (1997), and Bermúdez 1998. The essays in Eilan et al. 1993 give philosophical and psychological perspectives on spatial representation.

[8] See O'Keefe and Nadel 1978 and Gallistel 1990 for influential discussions and Filimon 2015 for an up-to-date (and skeptical) review of theory and data from across the cognitive, behavioral, and neural sciences.

explanatory projects. The first is explaining how a creature can arrive at an objective (perceptual) representation of the physical environment. The second is the project of explaining how a creature can arrive at an understanding that they inhabit an objective world of mind-independent objects. He points out, with some justice, that Strawson and Evans both slide imperceptibly from one to the other at important moments. For that reason, Burge claims, they both over-intellectualize the requirements of objective representation and make them dependent upon a relatively high-level conceptual apparatus. My account of the sense of "I," however, is plainly aligned with the second project, not the first, which is why the phylogenetic concern is not relevant—and also why Burge's own highly critical discussion of Evans's objectivity requirement is not directly relevant to my argument.

Some background. In addition to his discussion of self-reference and "I" Evans also claims that the very possibility of demonstrative reference and perceptual thought requires thinkers to be able to calibrate egocentric and allocentric representations. Burge takes issue with this aspect of Evan's thought and sees his arguments as prime examples of the conflation discussed above. I am sympathetic to Burge's position and his objections to Evans's arguments are telling. But placing an egocentric/allocentric calibration requirement on intentional self-reference is much more plausible than placing it on thought about ordinary physical objects. Understanding sentences involving "I" is a matter of grasping the truth conditions of thoughts about oneself. So it requires being able to think of oneself as a physical object among other physical objects, which in turn requires (i) a conception of the spatial relations between physical objects in general; (ii) a conception of one's own location in space; and (iii) a conception of how (i) and (ii) fit together. Evans's great insight into self-reference and self-consciousness is that (iii) is required so that we can express and understand thoughts about ourselves that are not purely egocentric. In contrast, Burge may well be right that none of

(i) through (iii) is a plausible requirement upon objective representation per se.[9]

In sum, abilities for self-location are fundamental to the cognitive role of "I." Moreover, these abilities are demanding. It can be a substantial achievement to calibrate one's egocentric path through the world with a non-egocentric representation of that very same path. Think back to Oedipus's moment of revelation. What he comes to realize is that his personal history, his egocentric path through space-time, can be viewed from a completely different perspective on which it is identical to the personal history of a man who killed his father and married his mother.

6.2. Meeting the Five Constraints

The first constraint is Essential Indexicality. Following Perry I argued that the informational difference between grasping the thought "I am F" and grasping the thought "JLB is F" is that the former, but not the latter, necessarily brings with it self-locating information. On the proposal put forward here this self-locating information comes because the thought "I am F" involves thinking of oneself under the mode of presentation *self*, where this engages the ability to locate oneself within the distal environment, calibrating one's egocentric perspective with a non-egocentric map of the world (a map that has a temporal dimension, as well as three spatial dimensions). So, when "I"-thoughts have immediate implications for action they do so as a function of the token-sense of "I."

A possible objection: Even granting that self-locating information is the key to essential indexicality, the proposed account seems to build too much into self-location. In order to grasp the thought

---

[9] But see Bermúdez 1995 and 1998, ch. 8 for what is in effect an argument that nonconceptual analogs of (i) through (iii) do hold for spatial representation at a phylogenetically more primitive level.

that I am being pursued by a bear, to continue with the well-worn example, I certainly need to apprehend that I am directly in the path of a bear, but that is purely egocentric self-location. Neither grasping the thought nor acting upon it requires me to think objectively or non-egocentrically about the spatial relations between me and the bear. In fact, trying to do that might have dangerous consequences!

Certainly, if I see a bear following me aggressively then part of what I see is that the bear stands in a certain spatial relation to me, where this spatial relation is purely egocentric. This type of egocentric spatial framing is an important part of the content of visual perception (and indeed of perception in the other modalities). And, for most of us, seeing a bear in pursuit is enough to trigger the appropriate behavior. But this is not the type of situation that the thesis of Essential Indexicality is intended to illuminate. Essential Indexicality is a thesis about how beliefs motivate action and, reciprocally, how we should explain actions in terms of beliefs. It certainly does not require that all motivated behavior be motivated by beliefs, which is fortunate given the many direct links that exist between perception and action.[10] Nor does it imply that perceptions can only motivate actions if they have the same kind of content as beliefs. Again, this is fortunate given how strong the reasons are for thinking that perceptions have fundamentally different contents from the thoughts that are the content of beliefs and other propositional attitudes.[11]

This book focuses on the mode of presentation *self*, the sense of the first person pronoun. This is at the level of full-fledged conceptual self-consciousness. As I have emphasized both in earlier chapters and elsewhere, this sophisticated way of thinking of oneself is underpinned by many, more primitive forms of self-specifying

---

[10] See, for example, Evans 1985; Hurley 1998; O'Regan and Noe 2001; and Noe 2005.
[11] For an overview of debates about nonconceptual content with an extensive bibliography see Bermúdez and Cahen 2015.

information.[12] Full-fledged conceptual self-consciousness is grounded in multiple forms of nonconceptual self-consciousness. While it is very important to understand the connections between conceptual and nonconceptual self-consciousness, it is equally important not to conflate them. In particular, nonconceptual self-consciousness is perception-dependent in a way that conceptual self-consciousness is not.[13] To be nonconceptually self-conscious is to be in receipt of, and able to act upon, locally self-specifying information—that is, information about one's immediate bodily disposition and about one's spatial relation to the local environment. Nonconceptual self-consciousness is paradigmatically underpinned by somatic proprioception and by the outward-directed senses. Conceptual self-consciousness brings a degree of emancipation from that perception-dependence. It allows the thinker to act and form plans in ways that are not bound either by the present time or by the present location. Nor do those actions and plans have to be stimulus-driven. And, of course, as Evans points out, it allows thinkers to grasp thoughts about themselves that they neither decide nor offer grounds for.

So, to respond to the objection, while it is true that I can come to think "I am being pursued by a bear" by, in effect, taking my perception of a rapidly approaching bear at face value, an account of the abilities deployed in that thought needs to take account of the fact that that very same thought can be thought in very different and much richer contexts. I might, for example, come to think it by looking at a webcam on my phone and realizing that I myself am the person with the bear rapidly approaching behind him. Or I might realize that I fit the description that has just been broadcast by the park rangers of the person who is being surreptitiously tracked by a bear. These are both cases that bring Essential Indexicality into play. They both involve self-location, but do so in

---

[12] Bermúdez 1995, 1998, 2001a, 2001b, 2003b.
[13] Compare the distinction between level-1 and level-2 self-consciousness drawn in Peacocke 2014.

a way that exploits my general ability to calibrate egocentric information and non-egocentric information, as per my general account of the token-sense of "I."

It is really only because the thought "I am being pursued by a bear" can occur in these richer contexts that notions of belief, sense, and content really come into play. Creatures whose engagement with the environment is purely driven by perception can at best be described as enjoying proto-beliefs.[14] Beliefs proper are perception-independent states. The same belief can be arrived at in multiple different ways—through reasoning, testimony, and imaginative simulation, for example—and the belief's content does not change as a function of how it was reached. For that reason the content even of a perceptually derived belief must be built up from components that are themselves perception-independent and that can feature in the contents of beliefs derived completely nonperceptually, which in turn is why almost all philosophers in this area hold that the constituents of belief contents are freely recombinable concepts (senses).[15] This has very clear ramifications for thinking about the sense of "I." Modulo the distinction between type-sense and token-sense there must be a unitary account of the sense of "I" that holds across all contexts in which "I"-thoughts can be expressed and understood. This requirement is an important element in distinguishing conceptual from nonconceptual self-consciousness, and it means that the sense of "I" must itself be understood in a perception-independent way, which is the driver for the proposed account of the sense of "I." What makes the thought "I am being pursued by a bear" a genuine thought (as opposed to a perceptual proto-belief) is that it engages a richer way of thinking of the self than can be found in the perception from which it is derived.

---

[14] See Bermúdez 2003a for further discussion.
[15] This requirement is voiced very differently by Jerry Fodor (1975) and Gareth Evans (1982).

I turn now to Truth Conditions, which requires accommodating the distinction between knowing in general terms what it would be for the sentence featuring the indexical to be true (without necessarily being able to identify the referent of the indexical) and knowing a specific truth condition (where this requires being able to identify the referents of the indexical). As suggested earlier, the general knowledge of a truth condition emerges at the level of type-sense, while the specific knowledge is a function of grasp of token-sense. My account makes clear how grasping the token-sense of "I" contributes to a practical capacity to determine the specific truth condition of sentences using "I" and for knowing how to go about determining the truth value of sentences about myself that cannot be immediately decided on the basis of information from information channels that have the IEM property. And even those sentences that can be so decided are sentences about a physical object located in space and following a single trajectory through space-time, and I cannot grasp their truth conditions without grasping that I myself am such a thing. That this is so follows from the nature of the information channels involved. Somatic proprioception, for example, presents information about the embodied self, while self-specifying bodily information is an integral part of exteroceptive perception, particularly in vision and touch. Moreover, as will emerge in more detail in Chapter 7, autobiographical memories are located within a personal narrative.[16]

Introspection may seem more challenging, however. In what sense is self-location required for beliefs about one's own mental states derived from introspection? There are two separate questions here. The first is whether there could be a disembodied thinker capable of thinking "I"-thoughts. I am agnostic on that

---

[16] I have defended these claims in more details elsewhere. For somatic proprioception see Bermúdez 2005a and 2011b; for vision see Bermúdez 1998, ch. 5; and for memory see Bermúdez forthcoming-a.

question.[17] It seems plain to me, however, that any such thinker would have very different "I"-thoughts from ours. So the relevant question is: How should we think about the sense of "I" in self-ascriptions of psychological states, given that we are presented to ourselves in multiple ways as physical objects moving on a single path through space and time? And the answer is: Exactly the same way that we think about the sense of "I" in other contexts. For reasons brought out earlier, "I" has the same sense across all the contexts in which it features. We can think of that sense as a highest common factor in self-conscious thought. That is, it needs to be rich enough to accommodate all the contexts in which "I" is used.

That leaves three constraints. Symmetry requires it to be possible within a specified context that what you say using "you" or "he" can be token-equivalent (say the same thing) as what I say using "I." On the face of it, however, this is not possible if we understand the token-sense of "I" in terms of an ability to situate oneself within a cognitive map of the world. How can that ability be exercised by anyone but me? Do we not find ourselves once again with a private and unshareable sense of "I"?

To see why not, recall the connection between grasping the token-sense of "I" and grasping the specific truth condition of a sentence involving "I." Someone else who understands sentences that I utter using "I" in the same context in which I utter them will, simply in virtue of understanding them, also gain knowledge of that specific truth condition. What my understanding of "I" contributes to my understanding of "I am F" is the ability to locate a particular person (who of course is me) in space and time in such a way that I would typically know how to go about determining whether or not I am F. Now consider your understanding of my utterance of "I am F." What you deploy in understanding my utterance of "I" is the ability to locate a particular person (namely, me) in such a way that you know how to go about determining whether

---

[17] See Peacocke 2014 for an affirmative answer.

or not that person is F. Of course, the way in which you go about determining whether I am F may be very different from how I go about determining whether I am F. The first person and second person ways of establishing F-ness may differ (more on this in Chapter 7), but that has no bearing on the relation between your understanding of "I" and my understanding of "I," both of which exploit single ability.

I do not have a position on how to individuate abilities in general. But in the case of goal-driven activities it often makes best sense from the perspective of psychological explanation to individuate them by their ends (just as it often does in the case of goal-driven actions, like the example considered earlier of saving me from the bear, which is something that both you and I can do simultaneously with completely different strategies and bodily movements).[18] This is particularly so in the case of locational and navigational abilities, which it seems highly plausible to individuate in terms of their targets. If we can both find our way to Symphony Hall from a range of different starting points then there is a clear sense in which we both possess the same ability (the ability to find our way to Symphony Hall), even if there is no overlap between any of our starting-points. The (self-)locating abilities in the sense of "I" offer another good example. My ability to locate myself is the same as your ability to locate me, because there is a single person who is the object of both abilities. Once again, we need to relativize to contexts. There are many circumstances in which two people might be trying to locate the same person, but where there is no temptation to think of them both exercising a single ability. Here, though, you and I are both exercising the same ability because we are both starting from a particular individual in a particular context (me in this room in the university, for example) and what we are each doing is situating that individual relative to a more general and non-egocentric

[18] See section 3.1.

understanding of space. Moreover, this ability is the same ability that you exercise in your understanding of your own utterance of "you are not F." When you contradict my utterance of "I am F" by saying "you are not F" we are both starting from a particular individual in a particular context, whom we both understand to have a particular location in non-egocentric space, and predicating contradictory properties of that person. This very same ability is exploited again when I understand your utterance of "you are not F." So, as required by Symmetry, if I am a in this situation we have $[self_a] = [you_a]$.

Since Symmetry entails Shareability, all that remains is Frege's Criterion, which requires that no two token-senses can be the same if it is possible for a rational thinker to take incompatible attitudes to them. The only potential difficulty is posed by those Symmetry contexts where the token-sense of "I" is the same as the token-sense of "you." So consider a case where "I am F" has the same sense as "you are F." This might be a case where, for example, I learn that I am F through your telling me "you are F." Brief reflection shows that, on the account of token-sense proposed, no rational thinker could take incompatible attitudes to these two utterances. If "I am F" and "you are F" have the same sense then, plainly, the two utterances are saying the same thing about the person picked out by the utterances of "I" and "you." But if this is an occasion on which "I" and "you" express the same sense then, on the account proposed here, anyone who understands both utterances must be thinking about the same individual, namely me, in the same way. Any such thinker must be exercising a single capacity, the capacity to locate me. But if the two utterances both say the same thing about an individual that they each pick out in the same way, then there is no gap for her rationally to take different attitudes to the two utterances, and hence no way of applying Frege's Criterion to argue that the two sentences express different thoughts (at the level of token-sense).

6.3. The Type-Sense of "I" and Levels of Understanding

The discussion so far has emphasized the connections between type-sense and conventional linguistic meaning. This way of thinking about type-sense allows us to do justice to two apparently conflicting strands in the broadly Fregean notion of sense. On the one hand, it seems undeniable that the notion of sense has close connections with our understanding of language. At a minimum a thought is the sense of the assertoric sentence that gives its content, and so it is natural to equate understanding a sentence with grasping the thought that it expresses. On the other hand, though, the concept of sense that emerges from Frege's writings on the subject is deeply normative and rationalistic in ways that Burge has brought out.[19] There are different ways of thinking about the normativity of Fregean sense, but it is hard to disagree with Burge's insistence that the achievement of fully grasping a sense significantly outstrips simply knowing and being able to exploit conventional linguistic meaning. To put it another way, there are demands upon fully grasping the sense of a linguistic expression that go over and above understanding that expression's linguistic meaning. At least in the case of "I" and other indexicals, the distinction between type-sense and token-sense offers a way of capturing this basic insight, if type-sense is understood in terms of conventional linguistic meaning.

So what then is the type-sense of "I"? Chapter 5 showed that the type-sense/token-sense distinction cannot be mapped onto Kaplan's influential distinction between character and content. But that does not rule out the possibility of explaining type-sense in terms of Kaplan's character. Here again is Kaplan's statement of the meaning (character) of "I."

---

[19] See the essays in Burge 2005, particularly Burge 1990.

(D1) "I" is an indexical, different utterances of which may have different contents.
(D2) "I" is, in each of its utterances, directly referential
(D3) In each of its utterances, "I" refers to the person who utters it.[20]

I do not think, however, that (D1) and (D2) have any place in an account of conventional linguistic meaning. This is clear for (D2), since "directly referential" is a technical term known only to a few philosophers of language. In (D1) "indexical" is likewise a technical term and taking it out leaves us with nothing that is not already contained in (D3), namely the idea that the referent of "I" varies according to the person uttering it. So we are left only with (D3).

But (D3) does not really capture the conventional linguistic meaning of "I." For one thing, (D3) would be a perfectly accurate description of Anscombe's name "A" that every individual in her imaginary society has stamped on the inside of their wrist and that they use to refer to themselves non-self-consciously. As observed in Chapter 1, "I" is a linguistic device that is intentionally self-reflexive and intentionally self-ascriptive, and both of these features are missing from (D3). But of course "intentionally self-reflexive" and "intentionally self-ascriptive" are no less technical terms of art than "directly referential" and "indexical." Can they be incorporated into a plausible meaning rule of "I"?

Mark Sainsbury offers a good candidate.

Meaning rule for "I" (Sainsbury)
English speakers should use "I" to refer to themselves as themselves.[21]

---

[20] Kaplan 1989, p. 520. For discussion of how well Kaplan's character captures the linguistic meaning of "I" see Braun 1995; Dever 2004; and Mount 2015. The criticisms raised in these papers are interesting, but largely orthogonal to the argument here, as is discussion of the so-called Answering Machine Paradox and related issues (Predelli 2005 and for a review Cohen and Michaelis 2013).

[21] Sainsbury 2011, p. 254.

I do not agree with the claims that Sainsbury makes on behalf of this meaning rule. He states, for example, that all there is to understanding a token utterance of "I" is applying the meaning rule for "I" to that utterance, and he explicitly repudiates the proposal to distinguish token-sense from type-sense because he thinks that his meaning rule can accommodate the Symmetry Constraint. Looking at his argument in more detail, though, it becomes clear that he is operating with a two-level account very similar to Kaplan's. He has the meaning rule, on the one hand, and a notion of truth conditional content on the other.[22] As we saw in Chapter 5, no such account can simultaneously satisfy Symmetry and Frege's Criterion. Nonetheless, as an account of the type-sense of "I," I cannot see how to improve on the basic idea of Sainsbury's account.[23]

There are different levels of understanding "I"-sentences. The minimal level, and a necessary condition for all more substantive levels, is given by applying the meaning rule for "I"—namely, understanding that someone has uttered "I" in order to refer to himself as himself. It is because this minimal level of understanding is being exercised that one can properly be said to understand utterances of "I" even where one has no access to the details of context, and hence no way of moving from linguistic meaning to truth condition. An example might be the case discussed in Chapter 5 where I stumble across a piece of paper in the street on which all that remains legible is the first line of a will ("I write this document in full possession of my faculties..."). I have no way to determine who wrote this and hence no way of fixing a specific truth condition, but in a general sense of course I know that the sentence is true just in case it was written by someone who

---

[22] For example. "To self-refer is not to invoke a special ego-distinctive content, but to stand in a special relation to a content available to all: only you can use 'I' to refer to yourself, but any of us can use other expressions to refer to you, and to express the very same content that you express" (Sainsbury 2011, p. 255).

[23] Of course, and I'm sure Sainsbury would agree, there is room for fine-tuning to deal with the kind of issues raised by the authors cited in n. 2 in this chapter.

intended to refer to himself/herself as himself/herself and at the time of writing was in full possession of his/her faculties.

One reason my understanding is general rather than specific is that I have no way of recognizing what might count as evidence for or against the sentence's truth, since I have no independent grip on to whom it is that the token of "I" refers. We need to distinguish between the context of utterance and the context of evaluation. Note that the context of evaluation is different from Kaplan's circumstance of evaluation, or what Lewis calls an index.[24] The circumstance of evaluation is the context relative to which an utterance is evaluated. The context of evaluation, in contrast, is the context in which the evaluation is made, which can be very different from the context of utterance and the circumstance of evaluation.

Truth conditions are typically fixed by the context of utterance, but if the context of evaluation is significantly different from the context of utterance then the person evaluating the utterance needs to have a sufficient grip on the truth condition to allow them to evaluate it. This gives another important reason why location abilities are important. Consider a case where I hear you utter the sentence "I am F." In the context of utterance I have no evidence one way or the other as to whether you are F. But my understanding of what it is for that sentence to be true might allow me at a later date (i.e. in a different context of evaluation) to assign a truth value to the sentence (or at least to change my level of credence in it) if I come across new evidence. But if I am to apply that new evidence I must be able to keep track of you across different possible contexts of evaluation. So we see that the location abilities fundamental to understanding "I" at the level of token-sense can in some cases be diachronic, allowing me to get

---

[24] See Lewis 1980. Predelli 2005 discusses the relation between context of utterance and circumstance of evaluation.

a grip on who you are so that I can reidentify you in subsequent contexts of evaluation.

This gives a new way of thinking about different levels and degrees of understanding, which in turn allows me to fulfill an earlier commitment. In section 5.1 I suggested that a powerful motivation for the type sense/token-sense distinction is that it allows us to accommodate the obvious fact that it is possible to understand utterances of "I" without knowing much if anything of the context of utterances, while leaving space for a substantive account of the sense of "I" that illuminates the connection between self-reference and self-awareness. It is the type-sense of "I" that is exercised in minimal cases of understanding, while the substantive account is given at the level of token-sense. What we see now is that the token-sense of "I" is also a gradated phenomenon (*pari passu* for the token-sense of other indexicals such as "you"), as a function of the complexity of the location abilities engaged. Complexity here can be understood in terms of the ability to keep track of the referent of the term across different contexts of evaluation, and hence the ability to see how different types of information available in different contexts of evaluation might count for or against the truth of the thought expressed.

At the bottom end of the spectrum these abilities might not extend at all beyond the original context of evaluation. Here is an example. I might be in a position, relative to a given context of evaluation, to think about the referent of an indexical in a way that allows me *only* to use information available in that context in assessing the truth value of the uttered sentence. Suppose, for example, that on a cloudy night in a park I overhear someone at a distance say "I am wearing my favorite brown jacket." This is a case in which the context of evaluation is identical to the context of utterance. I can see the person silhouetted against the skyline and so I am able to identify him. I know what the specific truth condition of his utterance is (namely, that the utterance is true if and only if the person located at such-and-such a distance and direction from me is indeed wearing a brown jacket that he prefers to all others). In the dark I cannot see the color of his jacket, but if circumstances were to change I would be perfectly able to evaluate the truth value of the utterance—if the jacket were illuminated by a flash of lightning, for example, or by a passing car headlight. I plainly meet the criteria for grasping the token-sense of "I." I can locate the utterer of the sentence in a way that makes manifest the specific truth condition of the utterance. But, despite being able to do all this, my grasp of the token-sense of "I" is minimal in the following sense. I can only pick the person out in this particular context of evaluation. I do not have a sufficient fix on the speaker to be able to recognize him in a different context—at the well-lit park entrance, for example. Contrast this with a case where I get a better view of the speaker. I still cannot see the color of his jacket, but I see enough of his face to be able to recognize him. This significantly expands the range of possible contexts of evaluation. I can now evaluate the utterance in any context where I can perceptually pick out the person I overheard and where I have reason to believe that he has not changed his jacket.

Being able to recognize someone certainly broadens available contexts of evaluation for a given context of utterance, but it still limits evaluation to those contexts where the referent of the indexical is perceptually accessible. There are many ways of extending this. For example, I might acquire information about someone that allows me to draw on the testimony of others to evaluate utterances long after the context of utterance or even the original context of evaluation. With the right kind of triangulation I can keep track of individuals who are no longer alive (for the purpose of evaluating statements that they made when they were alive). In sum, grasping the token-sense of an indexical utterance requires my being able to grasp a specific truth condition relative to a given context of evaluation, which in turn requires my being able to think about and locate the individual picked out by the indexical. The greater the number of contexts of evaluation made available by my grasp of the token-sense of the indexical, the richer and more sophisticated are the location abilities deployed in grasping the relevant token-sense.

The thesis that there are distinct levels of complexity and sophistication in the location abilities exercised in grasping the token-sense of an indexical is particularly significant when we think about the first personal understanding of "I," because it allows us to see how the gradated nature of objective self-awareness is reflected in the capacity for self-reference. To be objectively self-aware is to be aware of oneself as an object—to be able to take a third-person perspective on oneself. Objective self-awareness varies in richness according to the richness of that third person perspective. At the limit, to be able to take a third person perspective on oneself is to see oneself as an agent with a character and identity that evolve as a function of actions and plans; to grasp the narrative structure of one's life; and to be able to track that narrative as it has unfolded and will unfold over time and through the objective world.[25] Plausibly, the richest form of third person perspective on oneself has a social dimension and so requires a degree of interpersonal self-awareness.[26] The important point is that the richer this third person perspective is, the more contexts of evaluation one will have available for assessing "I"-thoughts.

There do appear to be possible levels of objective self-awareness where the number of available contexts of evaluation is minimal. This may be the case in patients suffering simultaneously from anterograde and retrograde amnesia. Anterograde amnesia typically blocks the creation of new memories after a traumatic event,

---

[25] See Campbell 1994 for further discussion of a linear (narrative) conception of time and its importance in self-consciousness.
[26] Peacocke 2014 denies that being able to take a third person perspective on oneself (what he calls perspectival self-consciousness) requires interpersonal self-consciousness, on the grounds that the third person perspective can be completely nonpsychological. I have taken a different view (Bermudez 1998, ch. 9). But any dispute here is orthogonal to my main point, which is that perspectival

while retrograde amnesia typically blocks access to memories formed prior to the initiating event. When the two forms of amnesia occur in combination, as they did most famously in the case of the musician Clive Wearing, the result is a temporal perspective on the self that can last literally only for seconds. This would seem to be a case where the context of utterance is almost always the only possible context of evaluation for "I"-sentences (or any other indexicals). Plainly, though, this is most emphatically not the norm for "I." Nor, as we learn from discussion of the cognitive dynamics of "now" and "here," is it the norm for other pure indexicals. Thinking about a time as now and a place as here typically engages sophisticated abilities in keeping track of places and times. One manifestation of this is our ability, originally remarked upon by Frege himself, to use "then" to express and evaluate in a subsequent context the same thought that was expressed in an earlier context of utterance using "now." The same holds for spatial indexicals such as "here" and "there."[27]

6.4. Summary

We now have an account of the token-sense of "I" that meets the five constraints that have emerged from previous chapters—Essential Indexicality, Shareability, Symmetry, Frege's Criterion, and Truth Condition. The account, which develops the objectivity component of Evans's account of the sense of "I," places self-location at the core of the token-sense of "I." In contrast, the type-sense of "I" is the conventional linguistic meaning of "I"—as

---

self-consciousness is richer with interpersonal self-consciousness than without it, and with this I suspect that Peacocke would agree.

[27] For more on cognitive dynamics see the essays in Dokic 1997 and Prosser 2005.

Sainsbury notes, "I" is the word that English speakers use to refer to themselves as themselves. An account of the sense of "I" with these two components does justice both to the connections between self-reference and self-awareness and to the different levels at which "I"-sentences can be understood.

7

Explaining Immunity to Error through Misidentification

This final chapter returns to the phenomenon of immunity to error through misidentification. Chapter 4 rejected Evans's suggestion that the sense of "I" is (partially) given by the thinker's sensitivity to self-specifying information from sources that are identification-free because they can only yield information about the subject. These sources include introspection, somatic proprioception, visual kinesthesis, and autobiographical memory. They underwrite distinctively self-conscious judgments that have the IEM property. The IEM property needs to be accommodated at the level of sense. The thought expressed by "my legs are crossed," based upon proprioception, is very different from the thought expressed by "JLB's legs are crossed" (which you might utter, for example, on the basis of seeing my legs crossed). Evans's account offers a very clear way of understanding why certain first person judgments have the IEM property. Now that we have rejected this way of thinking about the sense of "I" we need to find another approach to explaining why first person judgments distinctively expressive of self-consciousness have the IEM property.

The strategy that I propose comes in two parts. The first part, discussed in section 7.1, emerges from three basic and uncontroversial claims about sense and concepts. I suggest that we build sensitivity to IEM-generating types of information into the sense of the predicate, as opposed to Evans's strategy of building it into the sense of the first person pronoun. However, this strategy cannot be applied to a very important class of first person thoughts—namely, past-tense thoughts based on autobiographical memory. Section 7.2 explains the problem and offers an analysis of how these thoughts can have the IEM property. Section 7.3 extends this analysis to an account of how thinkers can grasp past-tense thoughts with the IEM property.

7.1. Accounting for Immunity to Error through Misidentification: A General Strategy

Recall the basic connection between sense and concepts. For Frege, predicative expressions refer to concepts, which are functions from arguments to truth values. But, abstracting away from this technical sense of "concept," we can think of the sense of a complete sentence (a thought) as built up from concepts corresponding to subsentential linguistic expressions. So there is a very close correspondence between grasping the sense of a linguistic item and mastery of the corresponding concept. The strategy that I will propose rests upon three relatively uncontroversial claims about concepts/senses.

First, an account of what it is to possess a concept (that concept's possession conditions) must incorporate an account of the thinker's understanding of the concept's application conditions (the conditions in which it is appropriate to apply the concept).[1] There are few (if any) concepts for which understanding their application conditions is sufficient for mastery. Mastering a concept typically also involves knowing which inferences are licensed by the

---

[1] The vocabulary of possession conditions is introduced and developed in Peacocke 1992.

applicability of a given concept, and on what grounds the applicability of a given concept can be inferred. Still, an understanding of the conditions in which a concept should be applied seems basic, particularly for observational concepts (those concepts that can be directly applied on observational grounds), and observational concepts play a very basic role in judgments with the IEM property. So, any account of what it is to possess a concept that might be directly applied in judgments with the IEM property will have to incorporate an account of that concept's application conditions.

Second, some concepts have application conditions exploiting sensitivity to certain types of information. Observational concepts are again a good example. Part of what it is to possess the concept *green* is to be disposed to apply that concept when presented with certain distinctive types of visual information—in other words, to be disposed to judge that something is green when it looks green.[2] For many concepts, of course, the information will not be sensory information. But, I will suggest, sensitivity to appropriate sensory information is part of the possession conditions for an important class of concepts that can be self-ascribed in judgments with the IEM property.

Third, certain types of concept have both first person and third person application conditions, so that different types of information are relevant depending on whether one is applying the concept to oneself or to someone else. This is a familiar idea for psychological concepts, which can be applied first personally on introspective grounds, or third personally through observing behavior. Think of pain, for example. If we could only apply the concept "– is in pain" on the basis of sensation it is mysterious how we would ever be able to judge that someone else is in pain, while it is plain that we do not typically judge that we ourselves are in pain by applying behavioral criteria. I suggest below that it holds in general for

---

[2] For a model account along these lines see Peacocke's proposal for the concept *red* at pp. 7–8 of Peacocke 1992.

concepts that can be directly applied on the basis of identification-free information sources.

These three basic claims suggest a general strategy for giving an explanation at the level of sense of how an important class of first person judgments can have the IEM property. There are two basic components to a judgment of the form "I am F." We can identify them in terms of two different conceptual abilities, one related to the concept *I* and the other corresponding to the concept of F-ness. Correlatively, we can decompose the mental act of judgment in this case into two elements. The first element is sensitivity to the presence of F-ness. The second is the self-attribution of F-ness. In the special case we are considering, F-ness is some property or characteristic of which we are aware through information channel(s) such that there is no gap between being sensitive to the presence of F-ness in that way and being sensitive to the presence of F-ness in oneself. My hypothesis, therefore, is that the transition from sensitivity to F-ness to self-attribution of F-ness is underwritten by the possession conditions of the concept of F-ness. Part of what it is for a thinker to have the concept of F-ness is simply that she be disposed to make an immediate self-attribution of F-ness when she becomes aware of the presence of F-ness in the appropriate way. So, for example, to have the concept of toothache is to be disposed immediately to judge that one has toothache when one feels pain of the right kind in one's tooth.

The strategy depends upon the concepts in first person judgments with the IEM property having both first person and third person clauses in their application conditions, reflecting the basic fact that the criteria for applying those concepts can be very different in the first and third person cases. This bifurcation is plainly there for psychological concepts. The criteria for applying to oneself the complex concept *thinking of Bavaria* can be very different from those for applying it to someone else. In the first case the thinker might be dependent upon the deliverances of introspection, while in the second case the criteria might depend upon verbal reports or other forms of behavior. Likewise for concepts that can be applied to oneself on the basis of somatic proprioception. The criteria for applying the complex concept *extending one's arm* are very different depending on whether one is applying it to oneself on the basis of proprioception or applying it to someone else on the basis of visual evidence.

This same bifurcation is also present, I suggest, in concepts that might typically be applied on the basis of visual proprioception. Consider the concepts *in front of* and *to the left of*, for example. Looking at two objects and determining that one is to the left of the other involves a different set of cognitive skills and abilities from looking at an object and determining that it is to my left. Likewise for the comparison between seeing that one object is in front of another and seeing that it is in front of me. One important indicator here is that the second case typically involves exploiting an egocentric frame of reference (centered on the body), while the first exploits an allocentric frame of reference (centered on some nonbodily physical object). The same point holds for basic motor concepts, such as *approaching* or *retreating*. These can be applied first personally on the basis of visual kinesthesis, or third personally on the basis of perceptual evidence. In all these cases we have a single concept applied in two different ways according to two different sets of criteria—in a first person way and in a third person way. This fundamental difference has to be reflected in the concept's application conditions.

There are certainly significant challenges in developing this general strategy into a fuller explanation of the IEM property. Suppose that, on the basis of somatic proprioception, I judge that my arms are folded. It is implausible that the possession conditions of the concepts *folded* or *crossed* include special first person clauses governing how they might be applied to one's arms or legs respectively on the basis of proprioceptive information. I am inclined to think that my judgment that my arms are folded is not best analyzed as an application of the concept *folded* to my arms. A better analysis, I think, would be that it is an application to me of the complex concept *having folded arms*, a complex concept that has first and third person application conditions, each drawing upon different types of information. It should be noted, though, that this proposal raises difficult questions about the relation between the complex concept and the simple concepts from which it is built up. If the simple concepts *folded* and *arm* do not have distinct first and third person application conditions, where does the bifurcation come from when those simple concepts are composed into a complex concepts?[3]

I hope to address these and other challenges in later work. For the moment let me summarize the general strategy that I am proposing. Thoughts do not have the IEM property simpliciter. They have that property relative to the grounds on which they are made. Such thoughts contain concepts/senses denoting properties whose presence is detected through information channels that can only provide information about one's own properties. We can call these *IEM-susceptible concepts/senses*. Our abilities to exploit such information channels as introspection, somatic proprioception, visual kinesthesis, and so on, is reflected in the possession conditions for IEM-susceptible concepts/senses. My hypothesis is that part of what it is to possess an IEM-susceptible concept is that one be disposed to apply it to oneself when one becomes aware of the relevant property through an appropriative information channel. Judgments have the IEM property because their contents include at least one IEM-susceptible concept/sense. The possession conditions of the concept/sense ensure that an error of misidentification is not possible, when

---

[3] The extent to which this is a problem depends on one's attitude to (a version of) the principle of compositionality, according to which understanding a complex concept is straightforwardly derived from one's understanding of the concepts from which it is derived. This principle is discussed critically in Robbins 2005 and Johnson 2006.

Explaining Immunity to Error through Misidentification ~ 133

that concept is applied in the appropriate first person manner, on the basis of identification-free information-sources.

This sketch of an account explains the sense of a sentence in terms of the concepts of which it is composed. Those concepts are themselves being explained in terms of their possession conditions. For this reason the argument assumes a close connection between how concepts/senses are individuated and what it is to possess/grasp then. Christopher Peacocke has proposed the following principle as a way of capturing this close connection.

Principle of Dependence
There can be nothing more to the nature of a concept than is determined by a correct account of the capacity of a thinker who has mastered the concept to have propositional attitudes to contents containing that concept (a correct account of "grasping the concept").[4]

The Principle of Dependence in effect reduces concept individuation to possession conditions. I am sympathetic to this idea, but for present purposes require only the weaker claim that there can only be a difference in concepts/senses where there is a difference in the conditions for mastery/grasp. Nonetheless, even this weaker claim effectively builds application conditions into concept individuation. Some might worry that this makes thoughts too fine-grained. Would it not, for example, make a concept applied as a function of first person application conditions different from a concept applied as a function of third person application conditions?

Not at all. To say that concepts are individuated by their possession conditions is not to say that they are individuated by the particular grounds or evidence on which they are applied. We are considering cases where a concept can be applied on a range of different grounds—some first personal, some third personal. Spelling out the full possession conditions for applying the concept

[4] Peacocke 1992, p. 5.

would make clear that the concept has disjunctive conditions of application. What makes it the case that a thought incorporates *this* concept is that it is applied on one of those grounds—namely, that the thinker satisfies one of the clauses in the disjunctive specification of application conditions. But it certainly does not follow that when two thinkers satisfy different clauses they are thinking different thoughts.

In fact, some of the considerations that we discussed in the context of the Symmetry Constraint in Chapter 4 come into play again here. We need it to be possible for you to have a thought, on one set of grounds, that effectively denies the thought that I have had on a completely different set of grounds. In a yoga class, for example, I might say "I am in the half lotus position," when I have my eyes closed and so am relying purely on proprioception and muscle memory. You can see, however, that my legs are just crossed and so you say: "You are not in the half lotus position. You just have your legs crossed." This is a case, I claim, where you and I both entertain exactly the same thought, but I assert it whereas you deny it. In this context the token-sense of "I" and the token-sense of "you" coincide. Moreover we each engage the same concept, even though we do so on different grounds.

We see, therefore, the outlines of a general strategy for explaining how judgments can have the IEM property. The Frege–Evans approach explains the fact that certain first person judgments have the IEM property through the sense of the first person pronoun—sensitivity to self-specifying information obtained through the relevant information channels is part of what it is to think about oneself in appropriately self-conscious ways. On this approach, in contrast, the explanatory work is being done by the possession conditions of the concepts that are being self-ascribed on the basis of the deliverances of certain information channels. In the next section we turn to a class of judgments with the IEM property for which a very different approach is required.

7.2. Autobiographical Memory and the IEM property: An Analysis

Autobiographical memory is a species of episodic memory, which is standardly opposed to procedural memory (exploited in skilled behavior, for example) and semantic memory (exploited in language use and other forms of tacit information storage). Episodic memories are grounded in the subject's personal experience and, as their name suggests, store information about episodes in that individual's life. They can be either specific or generic. A generic episodic memory can be a composite derived from a number of different episodes. I might have a generic episodic memory of boxing at university, for example—as opposed to a specific episodic memory of a particular boxing bout in a certain year. Autobiographical memories can be either generic or episodic. What distinguishes them within the broad class of episodic memories is that their object is the agent, her activities, and her properties—as opposed to events or people that she experienced. Autobiographical memories, it is often said, are "from the inside."

Unsurprisingly, given the significance of autobiographical memories within our cognitive and affective lives, they give rise to many different types of first person judgments, some but not all of which have the IEM property.[5] Some of these first person judgments are relatively easy to accommodate using the strategy sketched out in the previous section. These are the *explicitly recollective* judgments that have their information-source built into them. Suppose my judgment is that I distinctly remember having had lunch with the job candidate last week (where my grounds for judging this is a vivid autobiographical memory of the occasion). This judgment plainly has the IEM property. This can be captured through the possession conditions of the concept *remember*, which

---

[5] As In Chapter 3 I am prescinding from possibility of quasi-memories.

plausibly has a separate clause for applications based on episodic, autobiographical memories.

The problematic first person judgments are those based on autobiographical memories, but that do not explicitly convey that they are so based—namely, past-tense judgments of the form "I φ-ed" or "I was F," as opposed to "I remember φ-ing" or "I remember being F." Many such judgments have the IEM property. Suppose, for example, that I have an apparent autobiographical memory of walking towards the Duomo in Florence, where the memory recapitulates my perceptual experience of approaching the Duomo. The corresponding past-tense judgment may certainly be mistaken. I might really have been remembering the Duomo in Pisa. And I might adjust my judgment accordingly if I discovered that it was really Pisa rather than Florence. But I cannot be mistaken about who it is whom I seem to remember walking towards the Duomo in Florence.

Nonetheless, some past-tense judgments are susceptible to error through misidentification, even when derived from autobiographical memories. We can illustrate this through a past-tense version of one of Wittgenstein's examples from the *Blue Book*. Suppose that I was involved in an accident and on waking up in hospital I have a vivid memory of feeling a pain in my arm and seeing an injured arm by my side with a large bruise. This is plainly an autobiographical memory. It is suitably episodic and self-specifying. On the basis of that memory I form the judgment "My arm was bruised." As it happens, however, the bruised arm I saw was not my own and in fact the pain in my arm came from a fracture rather than a bruise. This is clearly an error of misidentification.

So, what grounds the immunity to error of past-tense judgments with the IEM property cannot simply be that they are made on the basis of autobiographical memory because not all judgments based on autobiographical memory have the IEM property. And the type of account sketched in the previous section plainly does not apply. There is no plausibility in the thought that any concepts (with the exception of the concept of memory, and other related concepts) have a clause in their possession conditions for applications based on autobiographical memory. So here we have an information channel (autobiographical memory) that underwrites the IEM status of a large class of first person judgments, but that cannot be accommodated in the same way. So how should we understand the IEM status of these judgments?

First we need some terminology. Because autobiographical memories are all episodic memories they must originate in some earlier experienced episode in the subject's personal history. Call that episode the *experiential basis* for the autobiographical memory. The experiential basis is causally connected to the subsequent memory image and serves as the principal warrant for the eventual judgment. It is true that the later, past-tense judgment may deploy concepts that the thinker did not have available at the time of the remembered episode—I may only now have the conceptual machinery to identify my remembered state of mind as one of *schadenfreude*, for example.[6] Moreover, at the time of the original experienced episode the experiential basis could have served as warrant for the *present-tense analog* of the eventual autobiographical memory judgment. This is the judgment that the agent either did or could have made by taking the experiential basis at face value. So, in the accident example considered earlier in this section, my original experience of feeling a pain in my arm and seeing a bruised arm is the experiential basis for my eventual autobiographical memory judgment "I bruised my arm in the accident." The present-tense analog that I could have (and perhaps did) form at the time of the original experience is the judgment "That's my bruised arm."

My proposal is that the immunity status of a past-tense judgment is grounded in its experiential basis in a way that exactly maps how that experiential basis grounds the immunity status of the

---

[6] This kind of case is discussed in Martin 1992.

presnt-tense analog. On this view, a past-tense judgment grounded in autobiographical memory has the immunity property if and only if its present tense analog has the immunity property.

An initial reason to be sympathetic to this proposal is that the past-tense judgment and the present-tense analog share the same warrant. Each is justified through the same experienced episode, and one might plausibly think that the same features of that experienced episode will settle the question of whether a judgment warranted by it has the immunity property irrespective of whether that judgment is in the present tense or the past tense. In the background here is a general thesis about the semantics of tense. This is the thesis, most crisply articulated in Prior's tense logic, that tense functions adverbially, as an operator on sentences.

> I want to suggest that putting a verb into the past or future tense is exactly the same sort of thing as adding an adverb to the sentence. "I *was* having my breakfast" is related to "I am having my breakfast" in exactly the same way as "I am *allegedly* having my breakfast" is related to it, and it is only a historical accident that we generally form the past tense by modifying the present tense, e.g. by changing "am" to "was", rather than by tacking on an adverb. In a rationalized language with uniform constructions for similar functions we could form the past tense by prefixing to a given sentence the phrase "It was the case that", or "it has been the case that" (depending on what sort of past we mean), and the future tense by prefixing "It will be the case that".[7]

On this view, sentences are, as it were, intrinsically in the present tense. To put a sentence's main verb in the past or future tense is, in effect, to prefix the sentence with an operator either of the form "It was the case that" or of the form "it will be the case that." Complex tenses can be constructed by iterating these two basic tenses. The future perfect ("it will have been the case that φ") is modeled as "it will be the case that it was the case that φ"), and the

---

[7] Prior 1968/2003, p. 13.

pluperfect ("it had been the case that φ") is modeled as "it was the case that it was the case that φ."[8]

Understanding tense adverbially in this way strongly suggests a fundamental identity of content between a past-tense judgment and its present-tense analog. If we assume that the past-tense judgment is in the past simple tense then it has the form "P(φ)" (where "P" is the "it was the case that" operator. The embedded content φ is, of course, the content of the present-tense analog. What we might term the nonadverbial content of the past-tense judgment is just the content of the present-tense analog. If the past-tense judgment embeds the present-tense analog in this way it is eminently reasonable to think that either the two judgments will both have the immunity property, or neither will. They differ only in the pastness operator and it is hard to see how that can either remove the immunity property from an embedded judgment that possesses it, or add the immunity property to a judgment that lacks it.[9]

The view that there is no difference in representational content between a past-tense judgment and its present tense analog sits very naturally with the view that memory is fundamentally preservative. If memory is a tool for preserving knowledge, rather than creating it, then we would expect there to be no intrinsic difference in representational content between an autobiographical memory judgment derived from an experienced episode in one's personal history and a present-tense judgment derived from that same episode.

To turn these general thoughts into an argument consider Figure 7.1. The basic proposal is that past-tense first person judgment is *identification-dependent* (i.e. lacks the IEM property) if and only if the corresponding present-tense analog is identification-

---

[8] The sentence operator view of tense brings with it a number of general difficulties and challenges, particularly with respect to the semantic value of the embedded sentence. See Evans 1985; Lewis 1980/1998; and King 2007.

[9] For another argument see Bermúdez 2013.

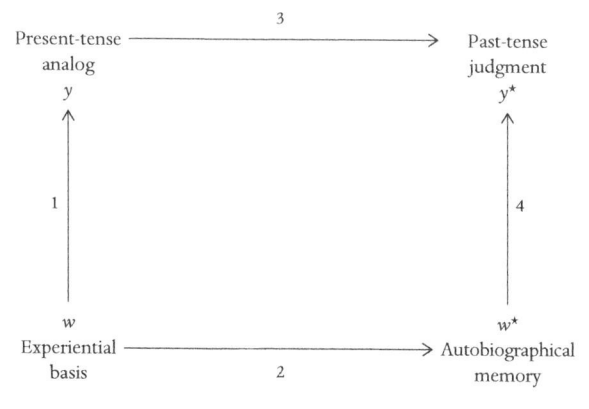

Figure 7.1 A schematic representation of the relations of warrant and grounding in past-tense memory judgments based on autobiographical memory.

dependent. A careful analysis of Figure 7.1 will show us how to establish this biconditional.

Figure 7.1 is a schematic representation of the relations of warrant and grounding that we have been discussing. Arrow (1) depicts the evidential relation between a present-tense analog y and experiential basis w. Experience w supports judgment y. Per arrow (2), experience w is the basis for the autobiographical memory w^*, in the sense that the informational content of w^* is the retained informational content of w. There is a parallel relation, depicted by arrow (3), between the present-tense analog y and the past-tense judgment y^*, in the sense that the content of y^* is a transformation of the content of y (as indicated further below). Finally, arrow (4) illustrates the evidential relation between the past-tense judgment y^* and the autobiographical memory w^* on which it is based.

There is no single arrow depicting the relation between the original experience w and the past-tense judgment y^*. This reflects the fact that the experience w can only support y^* through an epistemic intermediary. So far we have been primarily discussing

Explaining Immunity to Error through Misidentification ~ 141

the case where the epistemic intermediary is the autobiographical memory w^*, so that warrant is transmitted from w to y^* via the autobiographical memory w^*. The diagram illustrates an alternative evidential connection between w and y^*, however. On this alternative model, w supports the present-tense analog y, which in turn supports the past-tense judgment y^*. Here the epistemic intermediary would be the present-tense judgment y.

I will argue that Figure 7.1 represents a commutative diagram. That is, it depicts two (epistemically) equivalent "routes" between an experience w and a past-tense judgment y^*. This provides a powerful reason to accept the hypothesis that there is a two-way dependence between the identification-dependence of a past-tense judgment y^* and the identification-dependence of its present-tense analog y.

To see why, suppose that y is not IEM and assume for the sake of argument that the figure is indeed commutative. That means that the evidential relation depicted by arrow (1) must incorporate an anchoring identity judgment, as discussed earlier. So, to continue with Wittgenstein's example, if y is the judgment "I have a bump on my forehead" and w the experience of looking in a mirror, then w supports y only in the context of the identity judgment "I am the person in the mirror" or "I am *that* person" (where the demonstrative pronoun picks out the person in the mirror).

Looking at the diagram as a whole, it follows that this identity judgment is an essential component of the evidential relation between experience w and the eventual past-tense judgment y^* ("I had a bump on my forehead"). But then, since the diagram is commutative and the two routes from w to y^* epistemically equivalent, it follows that there must be a comparable identity judgment incorporated in the other route, namely, the route proceeding via the autobiographical memory w^*. There is no place for that matching identity judgment in the evidential relation captured by arrow (2). So it must be a part of the evidential relation depicted by arrow (4). To say that an identity judgment is implicated in the relation between the past-tense judgment y^* and the autobiographical memory w^* on which it is based, however, is simply to say that judgment y^* is identification-dependent, as required by the hypothesis.

An exactly parallel argument establishes the other direction of the biconditional. The identification-dependence of the past-tense judgment y^*, in conjunction with the commutativity of the evidential relations depicted in the diagram, requires the identification-dependence of the corresponding present-tense analog y.

The hypothesis seems justified, therefore, provided that we accept two lemmas. The first lemma is that Figure 7.1 is a commutative diagram, so that the clockwise and anti-clockwise routes track epistemically equivalent ways of grounding an experience-based past-tense judgment in its basing experience. The second lemma is that the relations plotted out in Figure 7.1 are essentially symmetrical.

I claim that the commutativity lemma is the only way of allowing for experientially-based past-tense judgments "I was φ-ing at t" to be justified in the absence of an autobiographical memory of oneself φ–ing at t. Many past-tense judgments about oneself are warranted on the basis of testimony, but testimony cannot provide warrant for experientially-based judgments. So, if commutativity fails, then there are really only two ways of warranting past-tense judgments about oneself. One form of warrant has its basis in experience as retained and transmitted through autobiographical memory. The other has its basis in testimony. But that is surely too narrow a way of thinking about past-tense first person judgments. I certainly seem to be able to make warranted past-tense judgments that are grounded neither in testimony nor in autobiographical memory.

To take a simple example, suppose that I am a restaurant critic and dine out far too often to have any reliable memories of what

I have eaten, where, and when. Even though my gustatory memories are blurred and gappy, all I need to do is to keep a note of dates, times, and meals as I experience them. This would allow me to make warranted past-tense judgments of the form "I had fillet of trout last Wednesday for lunch," even without any autobiographical memory of last Wednesday's lunch or eyewitness reports from other people in the restaurant.

In essence, the envisaged situation exploits the clockwise route in Figure 7.1—I make a present-tense judgment ("I am having fillet of trout for lunch") in my diary on Wednesday and use that as warrant for my subsequent past-tense judgment "I had fillet of trout for lunch on Wednesday." Certainly, someone with a better memory than me could have taken the anti-clockwise route to the same result. But they would be no better off than me (and, in normal circumstances, no worse off)—at least, epistemically speaking. That is all that commutativity requires. There may be all sorts of reasons for preferring memory to note-taking when it comes to restaurant meals, but (I submit) those reasons are not epistemic ones.

That leaves the symmetry lemma. The issue here is the relation between Arrow (2) and Arrow (3). Arrow (2) denotes the relation between an autobiographical memory and its experiential basis. Arrow (3) denotes the relation between a past-tense judgment $y^\star$ and its present-tense analog y. The basic reason for thinking that these two relations are symmetrical is that neither adds new informational content. In each case what we have is a content-preserving transformation. The content of an experience is preserved as the experience is retained, stored, and exploited in memory. Likewise, there is an identity of assertoric content between a past-tense judgment and its present-tense analog. The argument rests upon the earlier discussion of the logic of tense and the basic idea that memory judgments are fundamentally preservative.

To recap, in normal circumstances, the representational content of an autobiographical memory is straightforwardly derived from the representational content of the experience on which it is based. My memory of driving to work this morning is a function of the retained perceptual experiences that I enjoyed when driving to work this morning. Certainly, as Hume famously pointed out, memory images vary in their "force and vivacity," but that is not a difference in representational content. Moreover, remembering an episode autobiographically is much more than having in awareness a memory image or trace of that episode. It also involves being able to situate that episode within an autobiographical narrative. But that process of autobiographically framing the remembered episode is not part of the representational content of the memory in the strict sense. As we will discuss in the next section, it is part of how that autobiographical memory is integrated into the thinker's cognitive perspective on the world.

The basis for the symmetry lemma, therefore, is that the processes depicted by arrows (2) and (3) do not add any new informational content to their respective starting-points. Returning to the original argument for the hypothesis, the key step is that any anchoring identity judgment on one route from experiential basis to past-tense judgment must be matched by a parallel identity judgment on the other route. This yielded the conclusion that a past-tense judgment grounded in an autobiographical memory will be identity-dependent exactly when its present-tense analog is identity-dependent. Alternatively put, if there is an anchoring identity judgment in the relation depicted by arrow (1) then there must be a matching one in the relation depicted by arrow (4)—and vice versa. The argument for the symmetry lemma makes it even clearer why this has to hold. Since no representational content is added in the relations depicted by arrows (2) and (3), and since the figure is commutative, there must be a matching anchoring identity judgment and there is nowhere else for it to occur in the route from experiential basis to past-tense judgment.

In sum, explicitly recollective judgments all possess the immunity property. Judgments of the form "I remember φ–ing" can of course be mistaken, but not because one misidentifies oneself as the person whom one remembers φ–ing. Nonrecollective past-tense memory judgments do not invariably possess the immunity property. They possess it when, and only when, the recalled experiences are such that they would have warranted a present-tense judgment that would itself have had the immunity property. In this way, therefore, the immunity status of past-tense memory judgments is inherited from epistemic features of the original experience.

7.3. Understanding the IEM Status of Past-Tense Judgments

Judgments with IEM status have a distinct cognitive role and competent thinkers typically understand the different inferential roles of IEM and non-IEM judgments. As Crispin Wright has noted, for example, if an IEM judgment of the form "I am φ" is defeated, then it is not possible to retreat to the weaker claim "Someone is φ" in the way that one may with a judgment that is not IEM (Wright 1998). Competent thinkers typically respect this, which means that they must have some way of recognizing when judgments have the IEM property. They must be able to discriminate between past-tense judgments with the IEM property and past-tense judgments that lack it. This is a phenomenon at the level of sense because part of what it is to understand past-tense judgments made on the basis of autobiographical memory is to understand whether or not they have the IEM property. This phenomenon is easily explained in the case of the other types of judgment we have been considering (because it is plausibly built into the possession conditions of the relevant concepts). But how do we explain it in the case of past-tense judgments based on autobiographical memory?

The previous section proposed understanding the relation between past-tense judgments and their present-tense analogs through a general model of tensed judgments derived from Prior—a model on which the "pastness" of a past-tense judgment is analyzed in terms of an implicit quasi-adverbial modifier operating upon a present-tense judgment. Building on that proposal we can analyze what it is to understanding a past-tense judgment y* grounded in autobiographical memory in terms of two dissociable cognitive abilities:

(1) understanding y*'s present-tense analog y;
(2) understanding the pastness of the event reported by y.

So, we need an account of what it is to understand the pastness of a remembered episode. This will give us an account of the sense of the "pastness" operator, which is all that we specifically need for an account of the sense of a past-tense judgment, if we accept the general adverbial approach.

A starting point here is that specific (as opposed to generic) autobiographical memories are typically indexed to a certain point or period within the thinker's remembered personal history. And even generic autobiographical memories are typically experienced as memories of events that took place within a certain autobiographical time frame. An autobiographical time frame is a linearly ordered sequence of events in the life of a person. This is in contrast to the cyclical perspective on time that we find for example in a creature whose life is regulated by lunar cycles and the seasons.[10] An autobiographical narrative is not simply an

---

[10] See Campbell 1994 for extensive discussion of how a linear perspective on time contrasts with a cyclical one, and how it is integral to self-consciousness. The papers in Hoerl and McCormack 2001 are also very relevant.

ordered sequence of memories, however. It has a hermeneutic dimension—that is, it can incorporate an interpretation of the thinker's life in terms of goals and aspirations, realized or otherwise. It can have built into it information about the thinker's personal history that is not derived from memory. And of course it is likely to contain anticipations of the future, as well as plans.

There is no gap between autobiographically remembering an episode and locating that episode within one's own personal history. Having an autobiographical memory constitutively involves fitting it into an autobiographical narrative. The fit may be more or less precise. At one extreme memories can be dated (a memory of my last birthday party, for example). At another, they may simply fall within an extended autobiographical period (e.g. some time when I was a graduate student). But there are few, if any, autobiographical memories that carry no more historical specificity than being referred to a time earlier than the present and later than my birth.

Now, it is built into the project of developing an autobiographical narrative that it is the narrative of a single person. From the thinker's point of view, an experienced autobiographical narrative is identification-free. So, one might think that this is sufficient to explain how a thinker grasps the IEM status of first person judgments based on autobiographical memory. That would be a mistake, however. There are many things that go into an autobiographical narrative, and not all of them have IEM status. There are judgments based on autobiographical memory that lack IEM status, and simply fitting the basing memories into an autobiographical narrative cannot bestow that status upon them. If I entertain an autobiographical memory as part of an autobiographical narrative, then there can be no mistake about whose narrative it appears to be a part of. But that certainly does not secure the IEM status of judgments based on that autobiographical memory. The example adapted from Wittgenstein in the last section illustrates this point perfectly.

But we are nearly there. According to the earlier argument, the IEM status of a judgment based on autobiographical memory is coeval with the IEM status of its present-tense analog. No special account is needed of how a thinker grasps the IEM status of the relevant present-tense analogs because the relevant constraints upon inferential role are built into the possession conditions of the relevant concepts (as described above). So, in order to explain how thinkers grasp the IEM status of past-tense judgments we need to explain how they understand that IEM status is preserved by autobiographical memory. This is where integration of autobiographical memories into a personal history becomes key. It is true that such integration cannot bestow IEM status on memory judgments that do not have it. But it is equally true that such integration cannot take away the IEM status of an experiential basis that has it (or more precisely, of an experiential basis where the present tense analog has the IEM property). And any thinker who is aware of their autobiographical narrative as their own narrative will consequently grasp that IEM status is preserved in autobiographical memory.

7.4. Summary

This chapter has proposed a two-pronged strategy for explaining what it is to understand first person judgments with the IEM property. Everything depends upon the information source in play. For introspection, somatic proprioception, and visual kinesthesis, sensitivity to the relevant information-sources is built into the possession conditions of the predicative concepts/senses deployed in the judgment. First person judgments with the IEM property involve self-ascribing certain concepts on the basis of the deliverances of certain information-sources. Those concepts are such that one cannot grasp them without knowing how they should be self-ascribed on the basis of the relevant information. They are,

I conjecture, concepts that have both first and third person clauses in their possession conditions.

Autobiographical memory is more complicated, particularly when the judgments are simple past-tense judgments (I φ–ed), as opposed to explicit memory judgments (I remember φ–ing). Only some first person judgments based on autobiographical memory have the IEM property. I argued that such judgments have the IEM property exactly when their present-tense analogs have the IEM property, and developed a general account of how a thinker can understand the IEM status of past-tense. The key element of understanding a past-tense judgment is understanding the pastness of the relevant episode. On my account this in turn is a function of being able to situate that episode within an autobiographical narrative—within a personal history. The thinker's grasp of the IEM status of the past-tense judgment is partly derived from this, because it is built into the project of situating an episode within an autobiographical narrative that the narrative is the narrative of a single subject.

References

Adler, J. 2015. Epistemological problems of testimony. In Edward N. Zalta (ed.), *Stanford Encyclopedia of Philosophy* (Summer 2015 update). http://plato.stanford.edu/archives/sum2015/entries/testimony-episprob/ (accessd, Sep. 14, 2016).

Almog, J., J. Perry, and H. Wettstein (eds). 1989. *Themes from Kaplan*. Oxford: Oxford University Press.

Anscombe, G. E. M. 1975. The first person. In S. Guttenplan (ed.), *Mind and Language*. Oxford: Clarendon Press, pp. 45–65.

Armstrong, D. M. 1984. Consciousness and causality. In D. M. Armstrong and N. Malcolm (eds), *Consciousness and Causality*. Oxford: Basil Blackwell, pp. 105–91.

Bach, K. 2002. Giorgione was so-called because of his size. *Philosophical Perspectives* 16: 73–103.

Bell, D. 1979. *Frege's Theory of Judgment*. Oxford: Oxford University Press.

Bermúdez, J. L. 1995. Ecological perception and the notion of a nonconceptual point of view. In J. L. Bermúdez, A. J. Marcel, and N. Eilan (eds), *The Body and the Self*. Cambridge MA: MIT Press, pp. 153–73.

Bermúdez, J. L. 1998. *The Paradox of Self-Consciousness*. Cambridge, MA: MIT Press.

Bermúdez, J. L. 2001a. The sources of self-consciousness. *Proceedings of the Aristotelian Society* 102: 87–107.

Bermúdez, J. L. 2001b. Nonconceptual self-consciousness and cognitive science. *Synthese* 129: 129–49.

Bermúdez, J. L. 2005a. The phenomenology of bodily awareness. In D. W. Smith and A. L. Thomasson (eds), *Phenomenology and Philosophy of Mind*. New York: Oxford University Press, pp. 295–316.

Bermúdez, J. L. 2005b. Evans and the sense of "I." In J. L. Bermúdez (ed.), *Thought, Reference, and Experience: Themes from the Philosophy of Gareth Evans*. Oxford: Oxford University Press, pp. 164–94.

Bermúdez, J. L. 2005c. *Thought, Reference, and Experience: Themes from the Philosophy of Gareth Evans*. Oxford: Oxford University Press.

Bermúdez, J. L. 2011a. Self-knowledge and the sense of "I." In A. Hatzimoysis (ed.), *Self-Knowledge*. Oxford: Oxford University Press, pp. 226–45.

Bermúdez, J. L. 2011b. Bodily awareness and self-consciousness. In S. Gallagher (ed.), *Oxford Handbook of the Self*. Oxford: Oxford University Press, pp. 157–79.

Bermúdez, J. L. 2013. Immunity to error through misidentification and past-tense memory judgements. *Analysis* 73: 211–20.

Bermúdez, J. L. forthcoming-a. Yes, essential indexicals really are essential. *Analysis*.

Bermúdez, J. L. forthcoming-b. Memory and self-consciousness. Forthcoming in S. Bernecker and K. Michaelian (eds.), *Routledge Companion to the Philosophy of Memory*. London: Routledge.

Bermúdez, J. L. and A. Cahen. 2015. Mental content, nonconceptual. In *Stanford Encyclopedia of Philosophy* (Summer 2015 update).

Bradley, D. J. 2012. Four problems about self-locating belief. *Philosophical Review* 121: 149–77.

Branquinho, J. 1999. The problem of cognitive dynamics. *Grazer Philosophische Studien Grazen* 56: 2–15.

Braun, D. 1995. What is character? *Journal of Philosophical Logic* 24: 227–40.

Burge, T. 1979. Sinning against Frege. *The Philosophical Review* 88: 398–432.

Burge, T. 1990. Frege on sense and linguistic meaning. In D. Bell and N. Cooper (eds), *The Analytic Tradition*. Oxford: Blackwell, pp. 30–60.

Burge, T. 2003a. Memory and persons. *Philosophical Review* 112: 289–337.

Burge, T. 2003b. Postscript to 'Sinning against Frege'. In T. Burge, *Truth, Thought, Reason: Essays on Frege*. Oxford: Oxford University Press, 2005, pp. 240–1.

Burge, T. 2005. *Truth, Thought, Reason: Essays on Frege*. Oxford: Oxford University Press.

Burge, T. 2010. *Origins of Objectivity*. Oxford. Oxford University Press.

Burgess, A. 2013. Metalinguistic descriptivism for Millians. *Australasian Journal of Philosophy* 91: 443–57.

Campbell, J. 1994. *Past, Space, and Self*. Cambridge, MA: MIT Press.

Cappelen, H. and J. Dever. 2013. *The Inessential Indexical: On the Philosophical Insignificance of Perspective and the First Person*. Oxford: Oxford University Press.

Cassam, Q. 1995. Introspection and bodily self-ascription. In J. L. Bermúdez, A. J. Marcel, and N. M. Eilan (eds), *The Body and the Self*. Boston: MIT Press, pp. 311–36.

Cassam, Q. 1997. *Self and World*. Oxford: Oxford University Press.

Castañeda, H.-N. 1966. 'He': A study in the logic of self-consciousness. *Ratio* 8: 130–57.

Castañeda, H.-N. 1969/1994. On the phenomeno-logic of the I. In Q. Cassam (ed.), *Self-Knowledge*. Oxford: Oxford University Press, pp. 160–6.

Cohen, J., and E. Michaelson. 2013. Indexicality and the answering machine paradox. *Philosophy Compass* 8: 580–92.

Coliva, A. 2006. Error through misidentification: Some varieties. *Journal of Philosophy* 103: 407–25.

Corazza, E. 2004. *Reflecting the Mind: Indexicality and Quasi-Indexicality*. Oxford: Oxford University Press.

Dever, J. 2004. Binding into character. *Canadian Journal of Philosophy* 34: 29–80.

Dokic, J. 1996. *European Review of Philosophy, 2: Cognitive Dynamics* [special issue]. Center for the Study of Language and Information.

Donnellan, K. S. 1966. Reference and definite descriptions. *Philosophical Review* 75: 281–304.

Dummett, M. 1973. *Frege: Philosophy of Language*. London: Duckworth.

Dummett, M. 1981. *The Interpretation of Frege's Philosophy*. London: Duckworth.

Eilan, N., B. Brewer, and R. McCarthy (eds). 1993. *Spatial Representation: Problems in Philosophy and Psychology*. Oxford: Blackwell.

Evans, G. 1981. Understanding demonstratives. In H. Parret (ed.), *Meaning and Understanding*. Oxford: Clarendon Press, pp. 280–304.

Evans, G. 1982. *The Varieties of Reference*. Oxford: Oxford University Press.

Evans, G. 1985. Molyneux's question. In *Collected Papers*. Oxford: Oxford University Press, pp. 364–9.

Fagles, R. 1982. *Sophocles: Three Theban Plays*. Harmondsworth: Penguin Books.

Filimon, F. 2015. Are all spatial reference frames egocentric? Reinterpreting evidence for allocentric, object-centered, or world-centered reference frames. *Frontiers in Human Neuroscience* 9: 648.

Fodor, J. 1975. *The Language of Thought*. Cambridge, MA: Harvard University Press.

Forbes, G. 1987. Indexicals and intensionality: A Fregean perspective *The Philosophical Review* 96: 455–8.

Frege, G. 1892. On *Sinn* and *Bedeutung*. In M. Beaney (ed.), *The Frege Reader*. Oxford: Blackwell, pp. 151–71.

Frege, G. 1915. My basic logical insights. In G. Frege, *Posthumous Writings*. Trans. P. Long and R. White. Oxford: Basil Blackwell, pp. 251–2.

Frege, G. 1918a. Negation. In M. Beaney (ed.), *The Frege Reader*. Oxford: Blackwell, pp. 346–61.

Frege, G. 1918b. Thought. In M. Beaney (ed.), *The Frege Reader*. Oxford: Blackwell, pp. 325–45.

Gallistel, C. R. 1990. *The Organization of Learning: Learning, Development, and Conceptual Change*. Cambridge, MA: MIT Press.

Hamilton, A. 1995. A new look at personal identity. *Philosophical Quarterly* 45: 332–49.

Hamilton, A. 2007. Memory and self-consciousness: Immunity to error through misidentification. *Synthese* 171: 409–17.

Heck, R. 2002. Do demonstratives have senses? *Philosophers' Imprint* 2: 1–33.

Heck, R. G., Jr. 2005. Truth and disquotation. *Synthese* 142: 317–52.

Hoerl, C. and T. McCormack. 2001. *Time and Memory: Issues in Philosophy and Psychology*. Oxford: Oxford University Press.

Hurley, S. L. 1998. *Consciousness in Action*. Cambridge, MA: Harvard University Press.

Jack, J. 1993. The role of comprehension. In B. K. Matilal and A. Chakrabarti (eds), *Knowing from Words*. Dordrecht: Kluwer, pp. 63–193.

Johnson, K. 2006. On the nature of reverse compositionality. *Erkenntnis* 64: 37–60.

Kaplan, D. 1989. Demonstratives. In J. Almog, J. Perry, and H. Wettstein (eds), *Themes From Kaplan*. Oxford: Oxford University Press, pp. 481–563.

Katz, J. 2001. The end of Millianism. *Journal of Philosophy* 98: 137–66.

King, J. C. 2007. *The Nature and Structure of Content*. Oxford: Oxford University Press.

Kremer, M. 2010. Sense and reference: The origins and development of the distinction. In M. Potter and T. Ricketts (eds), *The Cambridge Companion to Frege*. Cambridge: Cambridge University Press, pp. 220–92.

Kripke, S. 1980. *Naming and Necessity*. Cambridge MA: Harvard University Press.

Lackey, J. 2008. *Learning from Words: Testimony as a Source of Knowledge.* Oxford: Oxford University Press.

Lackey, J. and E. Sosa. 2006. *The Epistemology of Testimony.* Oxford: Oxford University Press.

Lewis, D. 1979. Attitudes de dicto and de se. *The Philosophical Review* 88: 513–43.

Lewis, D. 1980/1998. Index, context, and content. In *Papers in Philosophical Logic.* Cambridge: Cambridge University Press, pp. 21–44.

Lewis, D. 1986. *On the Plurality of Worlds.* Oxford: Basil Blackwell.

Martin, M. 1992. Perception, concepts, and memory. *The Philosophical Review* 101: 745–63.

McDowell, J. 1977. On the sense and reference of a proper name. *Mind* 86: 159–85.

McDowell, J. 1993. Knowledge by hearsay. In B. K. Matilal and A. Chakrabarti (eds), *Knowing from Words.* Dordrecht: Kluwer, pp. 195–224.

McDowell, J. 1997. Reductionism and the first person. In J. Dancy (ed.), *Reading Parfit.* Oxford: Blackwell, pp. 230–50.

McKinsey, M. 1984. Causality and the paradox of names. *Midwest Studies in Philosophy* 9: 491–515.

McKinsey, M. 2010. Understanding proper names. *Linguistics and Philosophy* 33: 325–54.

Moore, A. W. 2003. Ineffability and nonsense. *Aristotelian Society Supplementary Volume* 77: 169–93.

Morgan, D. 2009. Can you think my "I"-thoughts? *The Philosophical Quarterly* 59: 68–85.

Mount, A. 2015. Character, impropriety, and success: A unified account of indexicals. *Mind and Language* 30: 1–21.

Newstead, A. 2006. Evans's anti-Cartesian argument: A critical evaluation. *Ratio* 19: 214–28.

Noë, A. 2005. *Action in Perception.* Vol. 102. Boston: MIT Press.

Nozick, R. 1981. *Philosophical Explanations.* Cambridge MA: Harvard University Press.

O'Keefe, J. and L. Nadel. 1978. *The Hippocampus as a Cognitive Map.* Oxford: Oxford University Press.

O'Regan, J. K. and A. Noë. 2001. A sensorimotor account of vision and visual consciousness. *Behavioral and Brain Sciences* 24: 883–917.

Oliver, A. 2010. What is a predicate? In M. Potter and T. Ricketts (eds), *The Cambridge Companion to Frege*. Cambridge: Cambridge University Press, pp. 118–48.

Parfit, D. 1984. *Reasons and Persons*. Oxford Oxford University Press.

Peacocke, C. 1981. Demonstrative thought and psychological explanation. *Synthese* 49: 187–217.

Peacocke, C. 1992. *A Study of Concepts*. Cambridge MA: MIT Press.

Peacocke, C. 2014. *The Mirror of the World: Subjects, Consciousness, and Self-Consciousness*. Oxford: Oxford University Press.

Perry, J. 1977. Frege on demonstratives. *Philosophical Review* 86: 474–97.

Perry, J. 1979. The essential indexical. *Philosophical Review* 86: 874–97.

Perry, J. 1997. Indexicals and demonstratives. In R. Hale and C. Wright (eds), *Companion to the Philosophy of Language*. Oxford: Blackwell, pp. 486–612.

Predelli, S. 2005. *Contexts: Meaning, Truth, and the Use of Language*. Oxford: Clarendon Press.

Prior, A. N. 1968/2003. *Papers on Time and Tense*. Oxford: Oxford University Press.

Prosser, S. 2005. Cognitive dynamics and indexicals. *Mind and Language* 20: 369–91.

Prosser, S. and F. Recanati (eds). 2012. *Immunity to Error through Misidentification: New Essays*. Cambridge: Cambridge University Press.

Pryor, J. 1999. Immunity to error through misidentification. *Philosophical Topics* 26: 271–304.

Quine, W. V. O. 1982. *Methods of Logic*, 4th edn. Cambridge MA: MIT Press.

Recanati, F. 1993. *Direct Reference: From Language to Thought*. Oxford: Blackwell.

Recanati, F. 2007. *Perspectival Thought: A Plea for (Moderate) Relativism*. Vol. 42. Oxford: Oxford University Press.

Ricketts, T. 2010. Concepts, objects, and the Context Principle. In M. Potter and T. Ricketts (eds), *The Cambridge Companion to Frege*. Cambridge: Cambridge University Press, pp. 149–219.

Ripley, D. 2011. Negation, denial, and rejection. *Philosophy Compass* 6.

Robbins, P. 2005. The myth of reverse compositionality. *Philosophical Studies* 125: 251–75.

Russell, B. 1918. The philosophy of logical atomism. In R. C. Marsh (ed.), *Logic and Knowledge*. London, 1956, pp. 177–281.

Sainsbury, R. M. 1979. *Russell*. London: Routledge Kegan Paul.

Sainsbury, R. M. 1998. Indexicals and reported speech. In R. M. Sainsbury (ed.), *Departing from Frege*. London: Routledge, pp. 137–58.

Sainsbury, R. M. 2011. English speakers should use "I" to refer to themselves. In A. Hatzimoysis (ed.), *Self-Knowledge*. Oxford: Oxford University Press, pp. 246–60.

Salmon, N. 1983. *Frege's Puzzle*. Cambridge, MA: MIT Press.

Salmon, N. 1989. Tense and singular propositions. In J. Almog, J. Perry, and H. Wettstein (eds), *Themes from Kaplan*. Oxford: Oxford University Press, pp. 331–92.

Salmon, N. 2002. Demonstrating and necessity. *The Philosophical Review* 111: 497–537.

Schiffer, S. 1981. Indexicals and the theory of reference. *Synthese* 49: 43–100.

Schwenkler, J. 2013. The objects of bodily awareness. *Philosophical Studies* 162: 465–72.

Shoemaker, S. 1968. Self-reference and self-awareness. *Journal of Philosophy* 65: 555–67.

Shoemaker, S. 1970. Persons and their pasts. *American Philosophical Quarterly* 7: 269–85.

Smiley, T. 1996. Rejection. *Analysis* 56: 1–9.

Soames, S. 1998. The modal argument: wide scope and rigidified descriptions. *Nous* 32: 1–22.

Stalnaker, R. C. 1997. Reference and necessity. In R. Hale and C. Wright (eds), *A Companion to the Philosophy of Language*. Oxford: Blackwell, pp. 534–54.

Strassler, R. 2009. *The Landmark Herodotus: The Histories*. New York: Anchor Books.

Strawson, P. F. 1959. *Individuals: An Essay in Descriptive Metaphysics*. London: Methuen.

Titelbaum, M. G. 2008. The relevance of self-locating beliefs. *Philosophical Review* 117: 555–606.

Travis, C. 2000. *Unshadowed Thought*. Cambridge MA: Harvard University Press.

de Vignemont, F. 2011. A self for the body. *Metaphilosophy* 42: 230–47.

Wittgenstein, L. 1953. *Philosophical Investigations*. Oxford: Basil Blackwell.
Wright, C. 1992. *Truth and Objectivity*. Cambridge, MA: Harvard University Press.
Wright, C. 1998. Self-knowledge: The Wittgensteinian legacy. In C. Wright, B. C. Smith, and C. MacDonald (eds), *Knowing Our Own Minds*. Oxford: Oxford University Press, pp. 13–45.

Index

abilities, individuating 117–18
action, explaining 47–50, 57, 103–5. *See also* essential indexicality; "I"-thoughts, role in explaining action
Anscombe, E. 8–9, 11, 120

Burge, T. 26, 28, 85, 109–11

Campbell, J. 52, 109, 147
Cappelen, Herman vi, 12–19
concepts, possession conditions of 129–35
Croesus 10–11

demonstratives 43, 45, 51–2. *See also* indexical expressions
Dever, Josh vi, 12–19
direct reference, theories of vi, 21, 31, 34, 45. *See also* reference; Russell/Mill theory of disquotational schema 5–7, 35–6
Dummett, M. 36, 44, 76–8, 103

essential indexicality vi, ix, 2, 12–19, 46–9, 88, 111–14. *See also* action, explaining
  Agency principle 11–12, 19, 20, 97
  Explanation principle 12, 13, 18, 20, 97
Evans, G. vi–viii, 26, 33, 41, 49, 67, 71, 80, 85, 140
  objectivity component vii, 57–60, 102, 107–10
  on sense of "I" vi–viii, 50–60, 62–6, 101–3, 113, 128
Expressibility Principle 2–7, 41

Frege, G.
  criterion for distinctness of thoughts 65, 72–3, 77–8, 89, 98, 118, 121

  on sense of "I" vi–vii, 43–5, 52, 56, 62–3
  on temporal indexicals 67, 126

Heck, R. 45, 76
Herodotus 10
Hurley, Susan v

"I"
  different analyses of "I am F," 23–4, 29–30
  intentionally self-ascriptive 8–10, 19
  intentionally self-reflexive 8–10, 19
  as linguistic device 7–8
  sense of "I" and sense of "you," 69–70, 72–3, 101–3, 135
  oken-sense of viii–ix, 84–95, 99–118. *See also* sense
  type-sense of viii–ix, 84–95, 119–21. *See also* Sense
identification-freedom/dependence 53–5, 68, 102, 134, 140–3, 148. *See also* Immunity to error
immunity to error through misidentification (IEM property) vii, ix, 53–6, 58, 101–2, 108, 115, 128–50. *See also* identiification-freedom
  general strategy for explaining 129–35
indexical expressions 43–50, 68–9, 70–1, 77, 82–6, 86–95
  character and content 48, 86–92, 119–20
"I"-thoughts 1–2, 7, 67
  objectivity of 62–6
  privacy of 62–3, 64, 66–7
  role in explaining action 46–50, 57. *See also* action, explaining; essential indexicality

Julius Caesar 9–12

Kaplan, D. viii, 25, 27, 43, 45, 48, 81, 86–92, 93–4, 100, 119–20, 122
King, J. 20–1, 140
Kripke, S. 21–2, 25, 27, 33, 45, 50, 85

Lewis, D. 3, 106–7, 122, 140

memory
  autobiographical ix–x, 55, 136–50
  episodic 136, 138
  judgments 137–50
Moore, A. W. 5
Morgan, D. 62–6, 76, 103–4

narrative, autobiographical 147–9

Oedipus 11–12

Peacocke, C. 100–3, 105, 113, 129–30, 134
Perry, J. viii, 11, 14, 16, 45–50, 54, 105–6, 111
  theories of content 45–50, 92–5
Prior, A. 139–40
proper names
  as metalinguistic descriptions 37–40
  Russell/Mill theory of 21–4, 45–6, 72–4, 86–7. *See also* direct deference, theories of understanding of 37–40, 81–2

reference, causal theory of 31–2

Sainsbury, M. viii, 37–8, 67–8, 70–1, 120–1
self-consciousness *See also* "I"-thoughts
  full-fledged/conceptual vi, 1–2, 112, 113–14, 125–6, 147–9
  nonconceptual v–vii, ix, 113
sense
  definite descriptions and 27–8, 32–3, 50
  determines reference 27–8, 32, 43, 50
  Frege's notion of vi, 20–34
  and linguistic understanding vi, 26–36
  as mode of presentation 28–9
  Token-sense vs. type-sense 81–6
Shoemaker, S. 53, 55–6
Stalnaker, R. 22, 27
Symmetry Constraint vii–ix, 62, 70–9, 98, 101–2, 105, 116–18, 121, 135
  and communication 75–8
  and denial, 72–5
  and same-saying 69–72

token-reflexivity 43
truth-conditions 27, 34–6, 65–6, 91–3
  circumstance of evaluation vs. context of evaluation 122–5
  grasping 82–5, 98, 99, 115–16, 121–3

Verificationism 35–6, 83

Wittgenstein, L. 4, 137
Wright, C. 146